50 *Fabulous* Knit Stitches

by Rita Weiss

Leisure Arts, Inc.
Little Rock, Arkansas

Produced by

Production Team

Creative Directors: Jean Leinhauser and
    Rita Weiss

Technical Editor; Ellen W. Liberles

Photographer: Carol Wilson Mansfield

Pattern Tester: Kim Britt

Book Design: Joyce Lerner

Published by Leisure Arts

© 2007 by Leisure Arts, Inc.,
5701 Ranch Drive
Little Rock, AR 72223
www. leisurearts.com

Introduction

Part of the pleasure of knitting is discovering and experimenting with beautiful new stitches.

And if you have been looking for new stitches to add creativity to your knitting projects, you've come to the right place. Here is a collection of 50 fabulous knit stitches which you can use in many different ways—for sweaters, for baby items, for afghans, for hats, even for socks—for anything you might want to create with your knitting needles.

What you won't find here is any reference to gauge. That's because you can work these stitches with any type or size of yarn you choose—from bulky to the finest lace weight. The patterns will look quite different, depending on the yarn you choose to use. Even your yarn color choices will make the patterns look different.

What you will find here is the word "multiple" at the start of each stitch pattern. A multiple is the number of stitches needed to work one complete unit of the pattern. If the pattern says "Multiple: 5 + 4", you will need to cast on any number of stitches which can be evenly divided by 5: 10, 15, 20, 25 or 30 for example. To this you need to add the "+4" so you will cast on 4 more stitches to the total, giving, for example 14, 19, 24, 29 or 34 stitches. **Important:** the "+" number is added just once.

Have fun swatching these patterns, then pick your favorites and start creating magic in your next project.

Contents

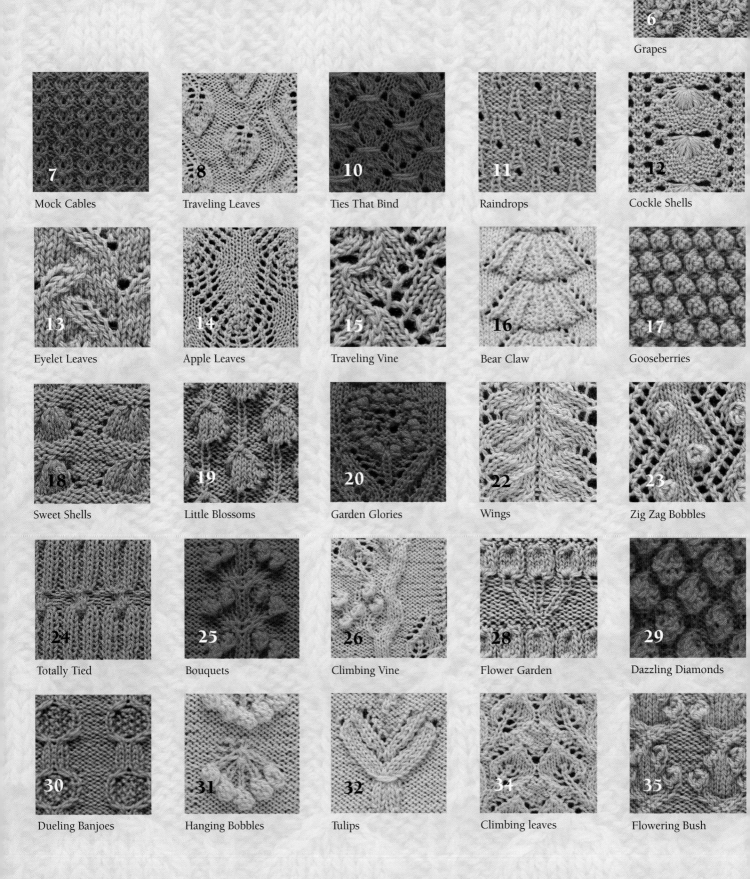

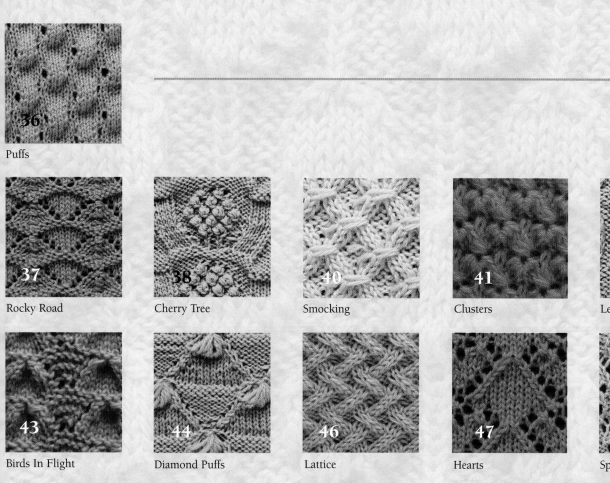

36

Puffs

37

Rocky Road

38

Cherry Tree

40

Smocking

41

Clusters

42

Leaves In A Row

43

Birds In Flight

44

Diamond Puffs

46

Lattice

47

Hearts

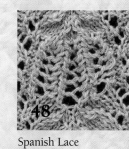

48

Spanish Lace

49

Beehives

50

Diamond Leaves

52

Chevron Bubbles

53

Leafy Columns

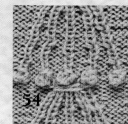

54

Petticoats

55

Arrowheads

56

Little Bells

57

Tassels

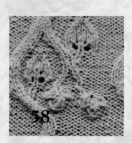

58

Flowering Vine

60

Hugs and Kisses

61

Sheaves of Wheat

62

Scallops

63

Puffys

GENERAL DIRECTIONS 64

5

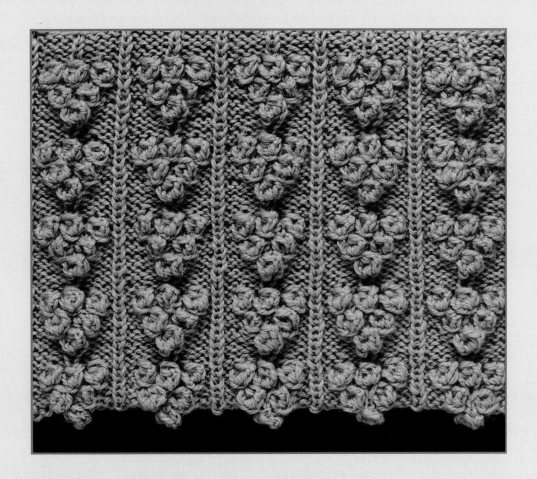

Grapes

Multiple: 10 + 3

STITCH GUIDE

BB (Bobble): [(K1, YO) twice, K1] into next st; turn; P5; turn; K5; pass 4th, 3rd, 2nd, and 1st st separately over the last st knitted: BB made.

INSTRUCTIONS

Row 1 (right side): K2; *P4, BB, P4, K1; rep from * to last st, K1.

Row 2: K1, P1; *K4, P1 (into BB), K4, P1; rep from * to last st, K1.

Row 3: K2; *P3, BB, P1, BB, P3, K1; rep from * to last st, K1.

Row 4: K1, P1; *K3, P1, K1, P1, K3, P1; rep from * to last st, K1.

Row 5: K2; *P2, BB, (P1, BB) twice, P2, K1; rep from * to last st, K1.

Row 6: K1, P1; *K2, P1, (K1, P1) twice, K2, P1; rep from * to last st, K1.

Row 7: K2; *P4, K1, P4, K1; rep from * to last st, K1.

Row 8: K1, P1; *K4, P1, K4, P1; rep from * to last st, K1.

Row 9: Rep Row 7.

Row 10: Rep Row 8.

Repeat Rows 1 through 10 for pattern.

Mock Cables

Multiple: 4 + 4

INSTRUCTIONS

Row 1 (right side): K1, P2; *K2, P2; rep from * to last st, K1.

Row 2: K3; *P1, YO, P1, K2; rep from * to last st, K1.

Row 3: K1, P2; *K3, P2; rep from * to last st, K1.

Row 4: K3; *P3, K2; rep from * to last st, K1.

Row 5: K1, P2; *K3, pass first st of sts just worked over last 2; P2; rep from * to last st, K1.

Repeat Rows 2 through 5 for pattern.

Traveling Leaves

Multiple: 22 + 2

STITCH GUIDE

M1 (Make one stitch): Pick up horizontal bar lying before next st and knit into back of this bar: Increase made.

P2SSO (Pass 2 sts over knit st): Slip 2 sts one at a time to right needle; then pass both sl sts tog over knit st: P2SSO made.

INSTRUCTIONS

Row 1 (wrong side): K1; *K3, P5, K4, P3, K7; rep from * to last st, K1.

Row 2: K1; *P5, P2tog, Knit into front and back of stitch, K2, P4, K2, YO, K1, YO, K2, P3; rep from * to last st, K1.

Row 3: K1; *K3, P7, K4, P2, K1, P1, K6; rep from * to last st, K1.

Row 4: K1; *P4, P2tog, K1, Purl into front and back of stitch, K2, P4, K3, YO, K1, YO, K3, P3; rep from * to last st, K1.

Row 5: K1; *K3, P9, K4, P2, K2, P1, K5; rep from * to last st, K1.

Row 6: K1; *P3, P2tog, K1, Purl into front and back of stitch, P1, K2, P4, sl 1, K1, PSSO, K5, K2tog, P3; rep from * to last st, K1.

Row 7: K1; *K3, P7, K4, P2, K3, P1, K4; rep from * to last st, K1.

Row 8: K1; *P2, P2tog, K1, Purl into front and back of stitch, P2, K2, P4, sl 1, K1, PSSO, K3, K2tog, P3; rep from * to last st, K1.

Row 9: K1; *K3, P5, K4, P2, K4, P1 K3; rep from * to last st, K1.

Row 10: K1; *P3, YO, K1, YO, P4, K2, P4, sl 1, K1, PSSO, K1, K2tog, P3; rep from * to last st, K1.

Row 11: K1; *K3, P3, K4, P2, K4, P3, K3; rep from * to last st, K1.

Row 12: K1; *P3, (K1, YO) twice, K1, P4, K1, M1, K1, P2tog, P2, sl 2, K1, P2SSO, P3; rep from * to last st, K1.

Row 13: K1; * K3, P1, K3, P3, K4, P5, K3; rep from * to last st, K1.

Row 14: K1; *P3, K2, YO, K1, YO, K2, P4, K1, knit into front and back of stitch, K1, P2tog, P5; rep from * to last st, K1.

Row 15: K1; *K6, P1, K1, P2, K4, P7, K3; rep from * to last st, K1.

Row 16: K1; *P3, K3, YO, K1, YO, K3, P4, K2, purl into front and back of st, K1, P2tog, P4; rep from * to last st, K1.

Row 17: K1; *K5, P1, K2, P2, K4, P9, K3; rep from * to last st, K1.

Row 18: K1; *P3, sl 1, K1, PSSO, K5, K2tog, P4, K2, P1, purl into front and back of st, K1, P2 tog, P3; rep from * to last st, K1.

Row 19: K1; *K4, P1, K3, P2, K4, P7, K3; rep from * to last st, K1.

Row 20: K1; *P3, sl 1, K1, PSSO, K3, K2tog, P4, K2, P2, purl into front and back of st, K1, P2tog, P2; rep from * to last st, K1.

Row 21: K1; *K3, P1, K4, P2, K4, P5, K3; rep from * to last st, K1.

Row 22: K1; *P3, sl 1, K1, PSSO, K1, K2tog, P4, K2, P4, YO, K1, YO, P3; rep from * to last st, K1.

Row 23: K1; *K3, P3, K4, P2, K4, P3, K3; rep from * to last st, K1.

Row 24: K1; *P3, sl 2, K1, P2SSO, P2, P2tog, K1, M1, K1, P4, (K1, YO) twice, K1, P3; rep from * to last st, K1.

Repeat Rows 1 through 24 for pattern. End by working Row 1.

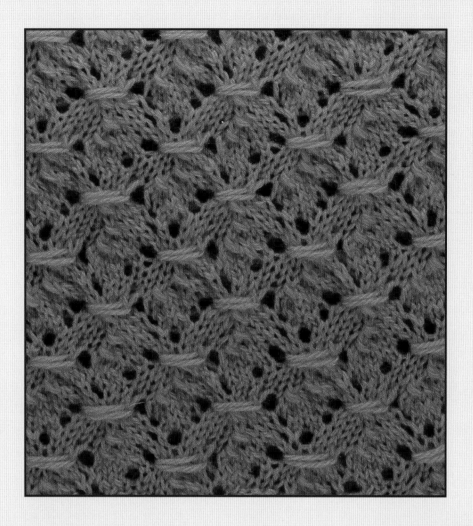

Ties That Bind

Multiple: 24 + 2

INSTRUCTIONS

Row 1 (right side): K1; *K1, YO, K4, sl 1, K2tog, PSSO, K4, YO; rep from * to last st, K1.

Row 2 and all even rows: K1, purl to last st, K1.

Row 3: K1; *YO, K3, sl 1, K2tog, PSSO, K3, YO, K3; rep from * to last st, K1.

Row 5: K1; *YO, insert right needle from front between next 7th and 8th sts on left needle and draw up a long lp; sl lp onto left needle and knit it tog with first st on left needle; then work wrapped sts as follows: K1, sl 1, K2tog, PSSO, K2; then continue with YO, K5; rep from * to last st, K1.

Row 7: K1; *(K4, YO, K1, YO, K4, sl 1, K2tog, PSSO) twice; rep from * to last st, K1.

Row 9: K1; *(K3, YO, K3, YO, K3, sl 1, K2tog, PSSO) twice; rep from * to last st, K1.

Row 11: K9; *YO, insert right needle from front between next 7th and 8th sts on left needle and draw up a long lp; sl lp onto left needle and knit it tog with first st on left needle; then work wrapped sts: K1, sl 1, K2tog, PSSO, K2; then YO, K5: rep from * to last 5 sts, K5.

Row 12: Rep Row 2.

Repeat Rows 1 through 12 for pattern.

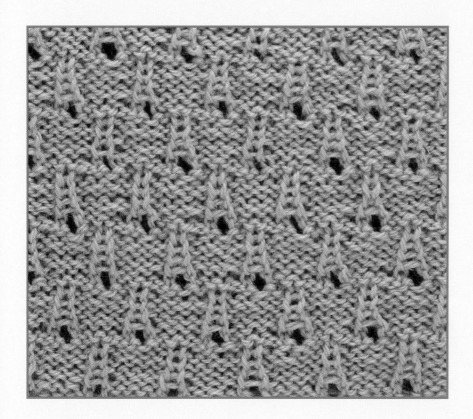

Raindrops

Multiple: 6+8

INSTRUCTIONS

Row 1 (right side): K1; *P4, YO, P2tog; rep from * to last st, K1.

Row 2: K2; *P1, K5; rep from *.

Row 3: K1, P4; *K1, P5; rep from * to last 3 sts, K1, P1, K1.

Row 4: : K2; *P1, K5; rep from *.

Row 5: K1, P4; *K1, P5; rep from * to last 3 sts, K1, P1, K1.

Row 6: K2; *P1, K5; rep from *.

Row 7: K1, P1; *YO, P2tog, P4; rep from *, ending with YO, P2tog, P3, K1.

Row 8: K5; *P1, K5; rep from *, ending with P1, K2.

Row 9: K1, P1; *K1, P5; rep from *, ending with K1, P4, K1.

Row 10: K5; *P1, K5, rep from *, ending with P1, K2.

Row 11: K1, P1; *K1, P5; rep from *, ending with K1, P4, K1.

Row 12: K5; *P1, K5, rep from *, ending with P1, K2.

Repeat Rows 1 through 12 for pattern.

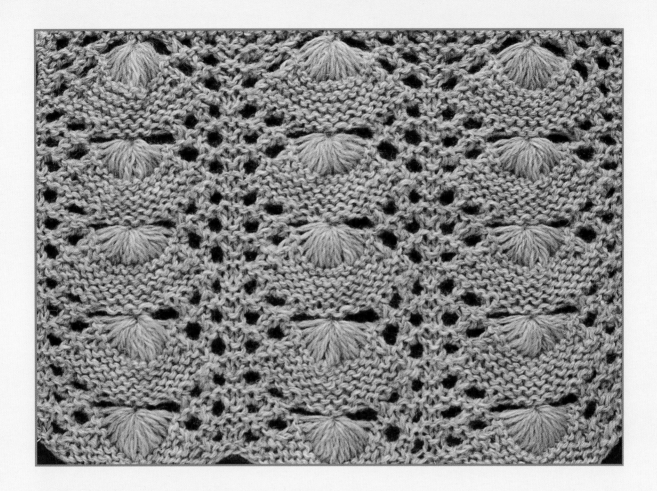

Cockle Shells

Multiple: 19 + 2

INSTRUCTIONS

Row 1: Knit.

Row 2 (right side): Knit.

Row 3: K1; *K1, YO, P2tog, K13, P2tog, YO, K1; rep from * to last st, K1.

Row 4: K1; *K1, (K1, P1 into YO), K15, (P1, K1 into YO), K1; rep from * to last st, K1.

Rows 5 and 6: Knit.

Row 7: K1; *K1, (YO, P2tog) twice, K11, (P2tog, YO) twice, K1; rep from * to last st, K1.

Row 8: K1; *[K1, (K1, P1 into YO)] twice, K13, [(P1, K1 into YO), K1] twice; rep from * to last st, K1.

Row 9: Knit.

Row 10: K1; *K6, (YO, YO, K1) 14 times, K5; rep from * to last st, K1.

Row 11: K1; *K1, (YO, P2tog) twice, YO, allowing extra lps to drop; sl next 15 sts to right-hand needle, then sl these 15 sts back onto left-hand needle and purl all 15 sts tog; (YO, P2tog) twice, YO, K1; rep from * to last st, K1.

Row 12: K1; *[K1 (P1, K1 into YO)] three times, K1, [(K1, P1 into YO), K1] three times; rep from * to last st, K1.

Row 13: Knit.

Repeat Rows 2 through 13 for pattern.

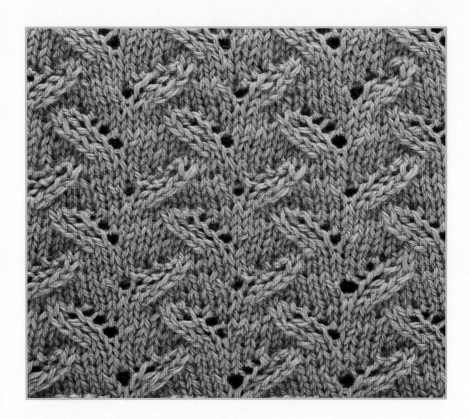

Eyelet Leaves

Multiple: 9 + 5

INSTRUCTIONS

Row 1 (right side): Knit.

Row 2: K1, purl to last st, K1.

Row 3: K4; *K2tog, K1, YO, K6; rep from * to last st, K1.

Row 4: K1, P1; *P6, YO, P1, P2tog; rep from * to last 3 sts, P2, K1.

Row 5: K2; *K2tog, K1, YO, K6; rep from * to last 3 sts, K3.

Row 6: K1, P3; *P6, YO, P1, P2tog; rep from * to last st, K1.

Row 7: Knit.

Row 8: K1, purl to last st, K1.

Row 9: K1; *K6, YO, K1, sl 1, K1, PSSO; rep from * to last 4 sts, K4.

Row 10: K1, P2; *P2tog tbl, P1, YO, P6; rep from * to last 2 sts, P1, K1.

Row 11: K3; *K6, YO, K1, sl 1, K1, PSSO; rep from * to last 2 sts, K2.

Row 12: K1; *P2tog tbl, P1, YO, P6; rep from * to last 4 sts, P3, K1.

Repeat Rows 1 through 12 for pattern.

Apple Leaves

Multiple : 19 + 2

STITCH GUIDE

SSK (slip, slip, knit): Slip next 2 sts as to knit, one at a time, to right needle; insert left needle into front of these 2 sts from right to left and then knit them tog: SSK made.

INSTRUCTIONS

Row 1 (right side): K1; *K4, (YO, SSK) 3 times, (YO, K2tog) twice, YO, K3, K2tog; rep from * to last st, K1.

Row 2 (and all even rows): K1, purl to last st, K1.

Row 3: K1; *K3, (YO, SSK) twice, YO, K2tog, SSK, YO, (K2tog, YO) twice, K4 ; rep from * to last st, K1.

Row 5: K1; *K2, (YO, SSK) twice, YO, K1, K2tog, SSK, K1, (YO, K2tog) twice, YO, K3; rep from * to last st, K1.

Row 7: K1; *K1, (YO, SSK) twice, YO, K2, K2tog, SSK, K2, (YO, K2tog) twice, YO, K2; rep from * to last st, K1.

Rows 9, 11, 13, 15: K1; *(YO, K2tog) twice, YO, K3, K2tog, SSK, K3, (YO, SSK) twice, YO, K1; rep from * to last st, K1.

Row 17: K1; *(YO, K2tog) twice, YO, K3, K2tog, K4, (YO, SSK) 3 times; rep from * to last st, K1.

Row 19: K1; *SSK, (YO, K2tog) twice, YO, K7, (YO, SSK) twice, YO, K2tog; rep from * to last st, K1.

Row 21: K1; *SSK, K1, (YO, K2tog) twice, YO, K5, (YO, SSK) twice, YO, K1, K2tog; rep from * to last st, K1.

Row 23: K1; *SSK, K2, (YO, K2tog) twice, YO, K3, (YO, SSK) twice, YO, K2, K2tog; rep from * to last st, K1.

Rows 25, 27, 29, 31: K1; *SSK, K3, (YO, SSK) twice, YO, K1, (YO, K2tog) twice, YO, K3, K2tog; rep from * to last st, K1.

Row 32: Rep Row 2.

Repeat Rows 1 through 32 for pattern.

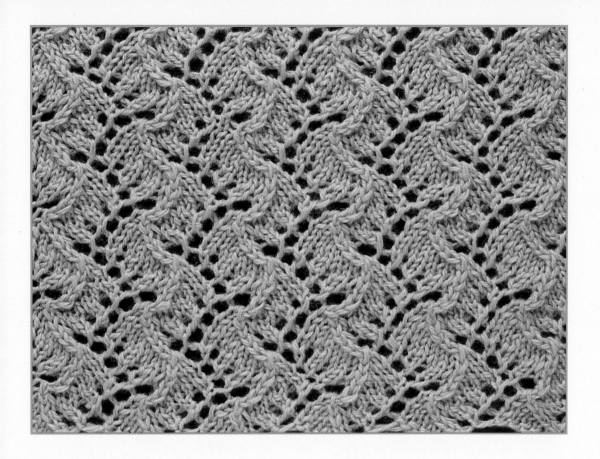

Traveling Vine

Multiple: 8 + 2

INSTRUCTIONS

Row 1 (right side): K1; *YO, K1 tbl, YO, sl 1, K1, PSSO, K5; rep from * to last st, K1.

Row 2: K1; *P4, P2tog tbl, P3; rep from * to last st, K1.

Row 3: K1; *YO, K1 tbl, YO, K2, sl 1, K1, PSSO, K3; rep from * to last st, K1.

Row 4: K1; *P2, P2tog tbl, P5; rep from * to last st, K1.

Row 5: K1; *K1 tbl, YO, K4, sl 1, K1, PSSO, K1, YO; rep from * to last st, K1.

Row 6: K1; *P1, P2tog tbl, P6; rep from * to last st, K1.

Row 7: K1; *K5, K2tog, YO, K1 tbl, YO; rep from * to last st, K1.

Row 8: K1; *P3, P2tog, P4; rep from * to last st, K1.

Row 9: K1; *K3, K2tog, K2, YO, K1 tbl, YO; rep from * to last st, K1.

Row 10: K1; * P5, P2tog, P2; rep from * to last st, K1.

Row 11: K1; *YO, K1, K2tog, K4, YO, K1 tbl; rep from * to last st, K1.

Row 12: K1; *P6, P2 tog, P1; rep from * to last st, K1.

Repeat Rows 1 through 12 for pattern.

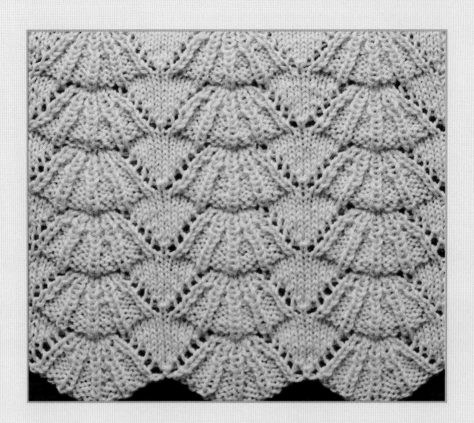

Bear Claw

Multiple: 18 + 2

INSTRUCTIONS

Row 1 (right side): K1; * K1, YO, (K1, P3) 4 times, K1, YO; rep from * to last st, K1.

Row 2. K1, *P2, (K3, P1) 4 times, P2; rep from * to last st, K1.

Row 3: K1; *K2, YO, (K1, P3) 4 times, K1, YO, K1; rep from * to last st, K1.

Row 4: K1; *P3, (K3, P1) 4 times, P3; rep from * to last st, K1.

Row 5: K1; *K3, YO, (K1, P3) 4 times, K1, YO, K2; rep from * to last st, K1.

Row 6: K1; *P4, (K3, P1) 4 times, P4; rep from * to last st, K1.

Row 7: K1; *K4, YO, (K1, P2tog, P1) 4 times, K1, YO, K3; rep from * to last st, K1.

Row 8: K1; *P5, (K2, P1) 4 times, P5; rep from * to last st, K1.

Row 9: K1; *K5, YO, (K1, P2tog) 4 times, K1, YO, K4; rep from * to last st, K1.

Row 10: K1; *P6, (K1, P1) 4 times, P6; rep from * to last st, K1.

Row 11: K1; *K6, YO, (sl 1, K1, PSSO) 4 times, K1, YO, K5; rep from * to last st, K1.

Row 12: K1, purl to last st, K1.

Repeat Rows 1 through 12 for pattern.

Gooseberries

Multiple: 2 + 5

STITCH GUIDE

M5: (P1, K1) twice, P1 in same st: 5 sts worked in one st.

wyf: with yarn in front
(on side of work facing you).

P2SSO: Sl 2, P1; pass slipped sts over purl st.

INSTRUCTIONS

Row 1 (right side): Knit.

Row 2: K2; *M5, K1; rep from * to last st, K1.

Row 3: K1; purl to last st, K1.

Row 4: K2; *sl 2 wyf, P3tog, P2SSO, K1; rep from * to last st, K1.

Row 5: Knit.

Row 6: K3; *M5, K1; rep from * to last 2 sts, K2.

Row 7: K1, purl, K1.

Row 8: K3; *sl 2 wyf, P3tog, P2SSO, K1; rep from * to last 2 sts, K2.

Repeat Rows 1 through 8 for pattern.

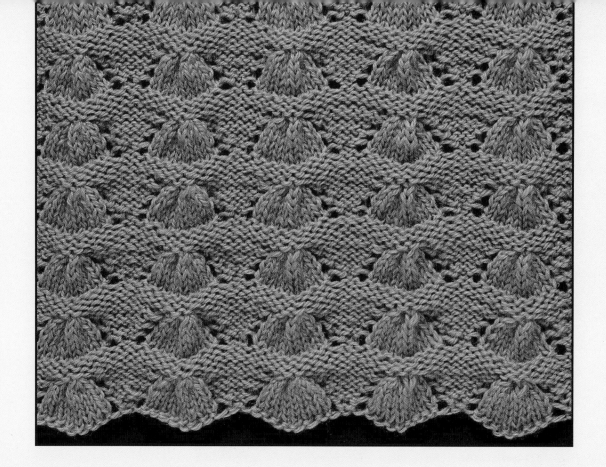

Sweet Shells

Multiple: 10 + 2

INSTRUCTIONS

Row 1 (right side): K1; *P1, YO, K8, YO, P1; rep from * to last st, K1.

Row 2: K1; *K2, P8, K2; rep from * to last st, K1.

Row 3: K1; *P2, YO, K8, YO, P2; rep from * to last st, K1.

Row 4: K1; *K3, P8, K3; rep from * to last st, K1.

Row 5: K1; *P3, YO, K8, YO, P3; rep from * to last st, K1.

Row 6: K1; *K4, P8, K4; rep from * to last st, K1.

Row 7: K1; *P4, (K4tog) twice, P4; rep from * to last st, K1.

Row 8: Knit.

Row 9: K1, purl to last st, K1.

Row 10: Knit.

Repeat Rows 1 through 10 for pattern.

Little Blossoms

Multiple: 10 + 6

INSTRUCTIONS

Row 1 (right side): K1, P4; *K1, P4, YO, K1, YO, P4 ; rep from * to last st, K1.

Row 2: K5; *YO, P3, YO, K4, P1, K4; rep from * to last st, K1.

Row 3: K1, P4; *K1, P4, YO, K5, YO, P4; rep from * to last st, K1.

Row 4: K5; *YO, P7, YO, K4, P1, K4; rep from * to last st, K1.

Row 5: K1, P4; *K1, P4, YO, K9, YO, P4; rep from * to last st, K1.

Row 6: K5; *P2tog, P7, P2tog tbl, K4, P1, K4; rep from * to last st, K1.

Row 7: K1, P4; *K1, P4, sl 1, K1, PSSO, K5, K2tog, P4; rep from * to last st, K1.

Row 8: K5; *P2tog, P3, P2tog tbl, K4, P1, K4; rep from * to last st, K1.

Row 9: K1, P4; *K1, P4, sl 1, K1, PSSO, K1, K2tog, P4; rep from * to last st, K1.

Row 10: K5; *P3tog, K4, P1, K4; rep from * to last st, K1.

Row 11: K1, P4; *YO, K1, YO, P4, K1, P4; rep from * to last st, K1.

Row 12: K5; *P1, K4, YO, P3, YO, K4; rep from * to last st, K1.

Row 13: K1, P4; *YO, K5, YO, P4, K1, P4; rep from * to last st, K1.

Row 14: K5; *P1, K4, YO, P7, YO, K4; rep from * to last st, K1.

Row 15: K1, P4; *YO, K9, YO, P4, K1, P4; rep from * to last st, K1.

Row 16: K5; *P1, K4, P2tog, P7, P2tog tbl, K4; rep from * to last st, K1.

Row 17: K1, P4; *sl 1, K1, PSSO, K5, K2tog, P4, K1, P4; rep from * to last st, K1.

Row 18: K5; *P1, K4, P2tog, P3, P2tog tbl, K4; rep from * to last st, K1.

Row 19: K1, P4; *sl 1, K1, PSSO, K1, K2tog, P4, K1, P4; rep from * to last st, K1.

Row 20: K5; *P1, K4, P3tog, K4; rep from * to last st, K1.

Repeat Rows 1 through 20 for pattern.

Garden Glories

Multiple 27+2

STITCH GUIDE

BB (Bobble): [K1, (YO, K1) 3 times] into next st: 7 lps on needle; pass 6th, 5th, 4th, 3rd, 2nd and 1st st separately over last st knitted; sl last st back to left-hand needle and K1: BB made

YRN (Yarn Around Needle): A YO before a purl st; bring yarn back over right-hand needle and forward between the needles: YRN made.

INSTRUCTIONS

Note: Yarn is carried in back for sl sts.

Row 1 (right side): K1; *K1, P1, sl 1, P1, K5, P2, K2, P1, K2, P2, K5, P1, sl 1, P1, K1; rep from * to last st, K1.

Row 2 (wrong side): K1; *(P1, K1) twice, P4, K3, P2, K1, P2, K3, P4, (K1, P1) twice; rep from * to last st, K1.

Row 3: K1; *K1, P1, sl 1, P1, K4, P2, K2tog, K1, YRN, P1, YO, K1, sl 1, K1, PSSO, P2, K4, P1, sl 1, P1, K1; rep from * to last st, K1.

Row 4: K1; *(P1, K1) twice, P3, K3, P3, K1, P3, K3, P3, (K1, P1) twice; rep from * to last st, K1.

Row 5: K1; *K1, P1, sl 1, P1, K3, P2, K2tog, K1, YO, K1, P1, K1, YO, K1, sl 1, K1, PSSO, P2, K3, P1, sl 1, P1, K1; rep from * to last st, K1.

Row 6: K1; *(P1, K1) twice, P2, K3, P4, K1, P4, K3, P2, (K1, P1) twice; rep from * to last st, K1.

Row 7: K1; *K1, P1, sl 1, P1, K2, P2, K2tog, K1, YO, K2, P1, K2, YO, K1, sl 1, K1, PSSO, P2, K2, P1, sl 1, P1, K1; rep from * to last st, K1.

Row 8: K1; *(P1, K1) twice, P1, K3, P5, K1, P5, K3, P1, (K1, P1) twice; rep from * to last st, K1.

Row 9: K1; *K1, P1, sl 1, P1, K1, P2, K2tog, K1, YO, K3, P1, K3, YO, K1, sl 1, K1, PSSO, P2, K1, P1, sl 1, P1, K1; rep from * to last st, K1..

Row 10: K1; *(P1, K1) twice, K3, P6, K1, P6, K3, (K1, P1) twice; rep from * to last st, K1.

Row 11: K1; *K1, P1, sl 1, P1, P2, (K2tog, K1, YO, K1) twice, YO, K1, sl 1, K1, PSSO, K1, YO, K1, sl 1, K1, PSSO, P2, P1, sl 1, P1, K1; rep from * to last st, K1.

Row 12: K1; *(P1, K1) twice, K2, P6, K1, P1, K1, P6, K2, (K1, P1) twice ; rep from * to last st, K1.

Row 13: K1; *K1, P1, sl 1, P1, P2, K3, K2tog, K1, YRN, P1, K1, P1, YO, K1, sl 1, K1, PSSO, K3, P2, P1, sl 1, P1, K1; rep from * to last st, K1.

Row 14: K1; *(P1, K1) twice, K2, P5, K2, P1, K2, P5, K2 (K1, P1) twice; rep from * to last st, K1.

Row 15: K1; *K1, P1, sl 1, P1, P2, K2, K2tog, K1, YRN, P2, K1, P2, YO, K1, sl 1, K1, PSSO, K2, P2, P1, sl 1, P1, K1; rep from * to last st, K1.

Row 16: K1; *(P1, K1) twice, K2, P4, K3, P1, K3, P4, K2, (K1, P1) twice; rep from * to last st, K1.

Row 17: K1; *K1, P1, sl 1, P1, P2, K1, K2tog, K1, YRN, P3, K1, P3, YO, K1, sl 1, K1, PSSO, K1, P2, P1, sl 1, P1, K1; rep from * to last st, K1.

Row 18: K1; *(P1, K1) twice, K2, P3, K4, P1, K4, P3, K2, (K1, P1) twice; rep from * to last st, K1.

Row 19: K1; *K1, P1, sl 1, P1, P2, K2tog, K1, YRN, P3, BB, P1, BB, P3, YO, K1, sl 1, K1, PSSO, P2, P1, sl 1, P1, K1; rep from * to last st, K1.

Row 20: K1; *(P1, K1) twice, K2, P1, K13, P1, K2, (K1, P1) twice; rep from * to last st, K1.

Row 21: K1; *K1, P1, sl 1, P1, P6, BB, P5, BB, P6, P1, sl 1, P1, K1; rep from * to last st, K1.

Row 22: K1; *(P1, K1) twice, P1, K17, P1, (K1, P1) twice; rep from * to last st, K1.

Row 23: K1; *K1, P1, sl 1, P1, K3, P2, BB, P1, P2tog, YRN, P2tog, YRN, P2, BB, P2, K3, P1, sl 1, P1, K1; rep from * to last st, K1.

Row 24: K1; *(P1, K1) twice, P3, K13, P3, (K1, P1) twice; rep from * to last st, K1.

Row 25: K1, *K1, P1, sl 1, P1, K3, P2, BB, (P2 tog, YRN) 3 times, P1, BB, P2, K3, P1, sl 1, P1, K1; rep from * to last st, K1.

Row 26: Rep Row 24.

Row 27: K1; *K1, P1, sl 1, P1, K3, P2, BB, P1, (P2tog, YRN) twice, P2, BB, P2, K3, P1, sl 1, P1, K1; rep from * to last st, K1.

Row 28: Rep Row 24.

Row 29: K1; *K1, P1, sl 1, P1, K4, P2, BB, P5, BB, P2, K4, P1, sl 1, P1, K1; rep from * to last st, K1.

Row 30: K1; *(P1, K1) twice, P4, K11, P4, (K1, P1) twice; rep from * to last st, K1.

Row 31: K1; *K1, P1, sl 1, P1, K6, P2, BB, P1, BB, P2, K6, P1, sl 1, P1, K1; rep from * to last st, K1.

Row 32: K1; *(P1, K1) twice, P7, K5, P7, (K1, P1) twice; rep from * to last st, K1.

Row 33: K1; *K1, P1, sl 1, P1, K8, P3, K8, P1, sl 1, P1, K1; rep from * to last st, K1.

Row 34: K1; *(P1, K1) twice, P19, (K1, P1) twice; rep from * to last st, K1.

Repeat Rows 1 through 34 for pattern. Where necessary, push bobbles through to right side.

Wings

Mutiple: 18 + 2

STITCH GUIDE

SKPO: Sl 1, K1, pass sl st over knit st: decrease made.

INSTRUCTIONS

Row 1 (right side): Knit.

Row 2: K1, purl to last st, K1.

Row 3: K1; *K8, P1, K8, P1; rep from * to last st, K1

Row 4: K2; *P8, K1, P8, K1; rep from * across.

Row 5: K1; *YO, K3, SKPO, K3, P1, K3, K2tog, K3, YO, P1; rep from * to last st, K1.

Row 6: K1; *K1, P1, YO, P3, P2tog, P2, K1, P2, P2tog tbl, P3, YO, K1; rep from * to last st, K1.

Row 7: K1; *K2, YO, K3, SKPO, K1, P1, K1, K2tog, K3, YO, K2, P1; rep from * to last st, K1.

Row 8: K1; *K1, P3, YO, P3, P2tog, K1, P2tog tbl, P3, YO, P3; rep from * to last st, K1.

Row 9: K1; *YO, K3, SKPO, K3, P1, K3, K2tog, K3, YO, P1; rep from * to last st, K1.

Row 10: K1; *K1, P1, YO, P3, P2tog, P2, K1, P2, P2tog tbl, P3, YO, P1; rep from * to last st, K1.

Row 11: K1; *K2, YO, K3, SKPO, K1, P1, K1, K2tog, K3, YO, K2, P1; rep from * to last st, K1.

Row 12: K1; *K1, P3, YO, P3, P2tog, K1, P2tog tbl, P3, YO, P3; rep from * to last st, K1.

Row 13: K1; *YO, K3, SKPO, K3, P1, K3, K2tog, K3, YO, P1; rep from * to last st, K1.

Row 14: K1; *K1, P1, YO, P3, P2tog, P2, K1, P2, SPPO, P3, YO, P1; rep from * to last st, K1.

Row 15: K1; *K2, YO, K3, SKPO, K1; P1, K1, K2tog, K3, YO, K2, P1; rep from * to last st, K1.

Row 16: K1; *K1, P3, YO, P3, P2tog, K1, P2tog tbl, P3, YO, P3; rep from * to last st, K1.

Repeat Rows 3 through 16 for pattern.

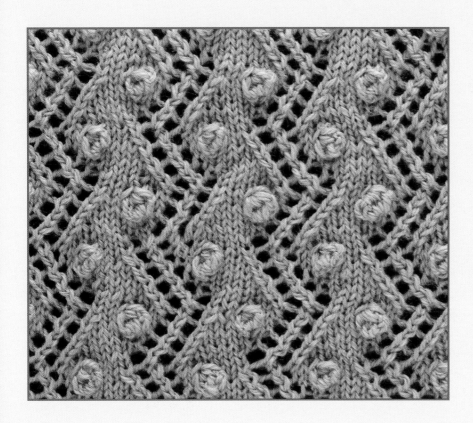

Zig Zag Bobbles

Multiple: 9 + 6

STITCH GUIDE

BB (Bobble): (K1, P1) twice, K1 into next st, turn; P5, turn; K5, pass 4th, 3rd, 2nd, and 1st st separately over the last st knitted: BB made.

INSTRUCTIONS

Row 1 (right side): K2; *(YO, sl 1, K1, PSSO) twice, K5; rep from * to last 4 sts, K4.

Row 2 and all even rows: K1, purl to last st, K1.

Row 3: K3; *(YO, sl 1, K1, PSSO) twice, K5; rep from * to last 3 sts, K3.

Row 5: K4; *(YO, sl 1, K1, PSSO) twice, K5; rep from * to last 2 sts, K2.

Row 7: K5; *(YO, sl 1, K1, PSSO) twice, K2, BB; K2; rep from * to last st, K1.

Row 9: K4; *(K2tog, YO) twice, K5; rep from * to last 2 sts, K2.

Row 11: K3; *(K2tog, YO) twice, K5; rep from * to last 3 sts, K3.

Row 13: K2; *(K2tog, YO) twice, K5; rep from * to last 4 sts, K4.

Row15: K1; *(K2tog, YO) twice, K2, BB, K2; rep from * to last 5 sts, K5.

Row 16: Rep Row 2.

Repeat Rows 1 through 16 for pattern.

TotallyTied

Multiple: 8 + 4

STITCH GUIDE

P-inc (Purl Increase): Purl into front of stitch, yarn back, purl into back of stitch: Increase made.

INSTRUCTIONS

Note:
Two cable needles (cn) are needed to work this stitch.

Row 1: K1; *(P2, K2) twice; rep from * to last 3 sts, P2. K1.

Row 2: K3, *(P2, K2) twice; rep from * to last st, K1.

Row 3: Rep Row 1.

Row 4: Rep Row 2.

Row 5 (right side): K1; * P2, sl 2 sts onto cn and leave at back of work; sl 2 sts onto second cn and leave at front of work; P next 2 sts tog; K2 from front cn; Ktog 2 sts from back cn; rep from * to last 3 sts, P2, K1.

Row 6: K3; *P4, K2; rep from * to last st, K1.

Row 7: K1; *P2, K4; rep from * to last 3 sts, P2, K1.

Row 8 (wrong side): K3; *sl 1 st onto cn and leave at front; sl 2 sts onto second cn and leave at back; P-inc, K2 from back cn, P-inc into st on cn at front; K2; rep from * to last st, K1.

Row 9: K1; *(P2, K2) twice; rep from * to last 3 sts, P2, K1.

Row 10: K3; *(P2, K2) twice; rep from * to last st, K1.

Rows 11 through 16: Rep Rows 9 and 10.

Repeat Rows 1 through 16 for pattern.

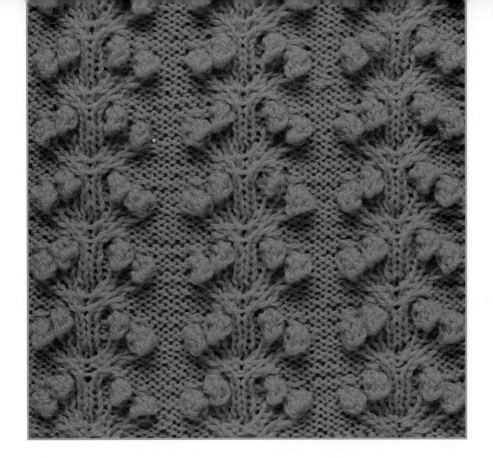

Bouquets

Multiple: 16+ 2

STITCH GUIDE

BC (Back Cross): Sl next st to cn and hold behind work; K1, then P1 from cn: BC made.

FC (Front Cross): Sl next st to cn and hold in front of work; P1, then K1 from cn: FC made.

C2F (Cable 2 Front): Sl next st to cn and hold in front of work; K1, then K1 from cn: C2F made.

C2B (Cable 2 Back): Sl next st to cn and hold in back of work; K1, then K1 from cn: C2B made.

BB (Bobble): (K1, P1) twice into next st, turn, P4, turn; K4, turn; (P2tog) twice, turn; K2tog: BB made.

INSTRUCTIONS

Row 1 (wrong side): K1; *K7, P2, K7; rep from * to last st, K1.

Row 2: K1; *P6, C2B, C2F, P6; rep from * to last st, K1.

Row 3: K1; *K5, FC, P2, BC, K5; rep from * to last st, K1.

Row 4: K1; *P4, BC, C2B, C2F, FC, P4; rep from * to last st, K1.

Row 5: K1; *K3, FC, K1, P4, K1, BC, K3; rep from * to last st, K1.

Row 6: K1; *P2, BC, P1, BC, K2, FC, P1, FC, P2; rep from * to last st, K1.

Row 7: K1; *(K2, P1) twice, K1, P2, K1, (P1, K2) twice; rep from * to last st, K1.

Row 8: K1; *P2, BB, P1, BC, P1, K2, P1, FC, P1, BB, P2; rep from * to last st, K1.

Row 9: K1; *K4, P1, K2, P2, K2, P1, K4; rep from * to last st, K1.

Row 10: K1; *P4, BB, P2, K2, P2, BB, P4; rep from * to last st, K1.

Repeat Rows 1 through 10 for pattern.

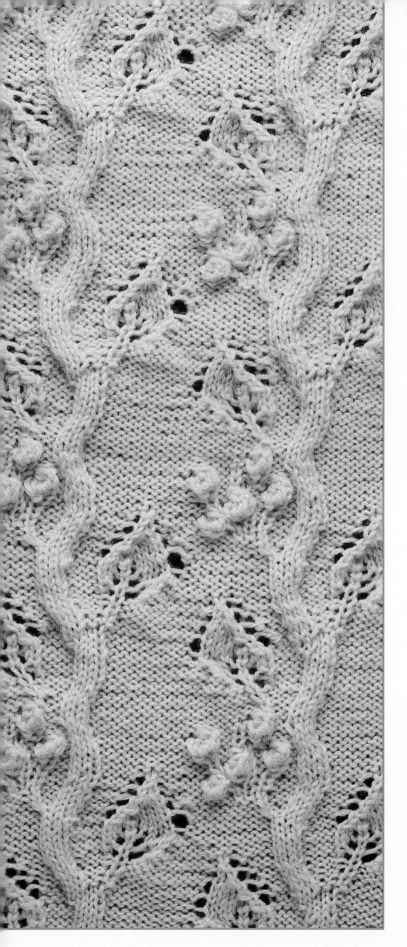

Climbing Vine

Multiple: 25 + 2

STITCH GUIDE

Cr4R (Cross 4 right): Sl one st to cn and hold at back, K3, P1 from cn: Cr4R made.

Cr4L (Cross 4 left): Sl 3 sts to cn and hold in front, P1, K3 from cn: Cr4L made.

Cr3L (Cross 3 left): Sl one st to cn and hold in front, P2, then K1 from cn: Cr3L made.

FC (Front Cross): Sl one st to cn and hold at front, P1, then K1 from cn: FC made

BC (Back Cross): Sl one st to cn and hold at back, K1, then P1 from cn: BC made

Bobble (BB): [(K1, YO) twice, K1] into next st, turn; P5, turn; K5, pass 4th, 3rd, 2nd, and 1st sts separately over the last st knitted: BB made.

INSTRUCTIONS

Row 1 (right side): K1; *P 11, K3, P2, K1, P8; rep from * to last st, K1.

Row 2: K1; *K8, P1, K2, P3, K11; rep from * to last st, K1.

Row 3: K1; *P10, Cr4R, P2, FC, P7; rep from * to last st, K1.

Row 4: K1; *K7, P1, K4, P3, K10; rep from * to last st, K1.

Row 5: K1; *P9, Cr4R, P4, YO, K1, YO, sl 1, K2tog, PSSO, P4; rep from * to last st, K1.

Row 6: K1; *K4, P4, K5, P3, K9; rep from * to last st, K1.

Row 7: K1; *P9, K3, P5, (K1, YO) twice, K1, sl 1, K2tog, PSSO, P2; rep from * to last st, K1.

Row 8: K1; *K2; P6, K5, P3, K9; rep from * to last st, K1.

Row 9: K1; *P9, K3, P5, K2, (YO, K1) twice, K1, sl 1, K2tog, PSSO; rep from * to last st, K1.

Row 10: K1; *P8, K5, P3, K9; rep from * to last st, K1.

Row 11: K1; P9, K4, P4, YO, sl 1, K2tog, PSSO, K5, YO; rep from * to last st, K1.

Row 12: K1; *K1, P6, K5, P4, K9; rep from * to last st, K1.

Row 13: K1; *P8, K1, P2, K3, P4, YO, sl 1, K2tog, PSSO, K3, YO, P1; rep from * to last st, K1.

Row 14: K1; *K2, P4, K5, P3, K2, P1, K8; rep from * to last st, K1.

Row 15: K1; *P7, BC, P2, Cr4L, P4, YO, sl 1, K2tog, PSSO, K1, YO, P2; rep from * to last st, K1.

Row 16: K1; *K3, P2, K5, P3, K4. P1, K7; rep from * to last st, K1.

Row 17: K1; *P4; K3tog, YO, K1, YO, P4, Cr4L, P4, YO, sl 1, K1, PSSO, P3; rep from * to last st, K1.

Row 18: K1; *K3, P1, K5, P3, K5, P4, K4; rep from * to last st, K1.

Row 19: K1; *P2, K3tog, (K1, YO) twice, K1, P5, K3, P9; rep from * to last st, K1.

Row 20: K1; *K9, P3, K5, P6, K2; rep from * to last st, K1.

Row 21: K1; *K3tog, K2, (YO, K1) twice, K1; P5, K3, P9; rep from * to last st, K1.

Row 22: K1; *K9, P3, K5, P8; rep from * to last st, K1.

Row 23: K1; *YO, K5, K3tog, YO, P4, K4, P9; rep from * to last st, K1.

Row 24: K1; *K9, P4, K5, P6, K1; rep from * to last st, K1.

Row 25: K1; *K1, YO, K3, K3tog, YO, P4, Cr4R, Cr3L, P7; rep from * to last st, K1.

Row 26: K1; *K7, P1, K3, P3, K5, P4, K2; rep from * to last st, K1.

Row 27: K1; *P2, YO, K1, K3tog, YO, P4, Cr4R, P3, K3, P5; rep from * to last st, K1.

Row 28: K1; *K5, P3, K4, P3, K5, P2, K3; rep from *to last st, K1.

Row 29: K1; *P3, K2tog, YO, P4, Cr4R, P3, BC, K1, Cr3L, BB, P2; rep from * to last st, K1.

Row 30: K1; *K3, P1, K2, P1, K1 P1, K4, P3, K5, P1, K3; rep from * to last st, K1.

Row 31: K1; *P9, K3, P3, BC, P1, K1, BB, P1, FC, P2; rep from * to last st, K1.

Row 32: K1; *K2, P1, K3, P1, K2, P1, K3, P3, K9; rep from * to last st, K1.

Row 33: K1; *P9, K3, P3, BB, P2, K2, P2, FC, P1; rep from * to last st, K1.

Row 34: K1; *K1, P1, K3, P2, K6, P3, K9; rep from * to last st, K1.

Row 35: K1; *P9, Cr4L, P4, K1, P1, K1, P3, BB, P1; rep from * to last st, K1.

Row 36: K1; *K5, P1, K1, P1, K4, P3, K10; rep from * to last st, K1.

Row 37: K1; *P10, Cr4L, P3, BB, P7; rep from * to last st, K1.

Row 38: K1; *K11, P3, K11; rep from * to last st, K1.

Repeat Rows 1 through 38 for pattern.

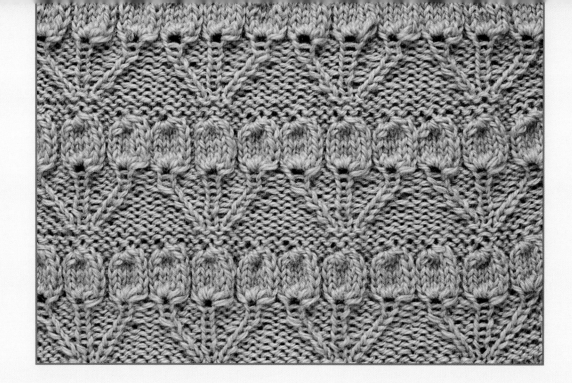

Flower Garden

Multiple: 11 + 2

STITCH GUIDE

FC (Front Cross): Sl one st to cn and hold in front, P1, then K1 from cn: FC made.

BC (Back Cross): Sl one st to cn and hold at back, K1, then P1 from cn: BC made.

M5 (Make 5): (K1, YO, K1, YO, K1) in same st: 5 sts in one made.

Dec 5 (Decrease 5): K5, pass 4th, 3rd, 2nd, 1st sts over: Dec made.

INSTRUCTIONS

Row 1: Knit.

Row 2: Knit.

Row 3 (right side): K1; *P4, K3, P4; rep from * to last st, K1.

Row 4: K1; *K4, P3, K4; rep from * to last st, K1.

Row 5: K1; *P3, BC, K1, FC, P3; rep from * to last st, K1.

Row 6: K1; *K3, (P1, K1) 3 times, K2; rep from * to last st, K1.

Row 7: K1; *P2, BC, P1, K1, P1, FC, P2; rep from * to last st, K1.

Row 8: K1; *K2, (P1, K2) 3 times; rep from * to last st, K1.

Row 9: K1; *P1, BC, P2, K1, P2, FC, P1; rep from * to last st, K1.

Row 10: K1; *K1, P1, (K3, P1) twice, K1; rep from * to last st, K1.

Row 11: K1; *P1, (M5, P3) twice, M5, P1; rep from * to last st, K1.

Row 12: K1; *K1, P5, (K3, P5) twice, K1; rep from * to last st, K1.

Row 13: K1; *P1, (K5, P3) twice, K5, P1; rep from * to last st, K1.

Row 14: Rep Row 12.

Rows 15 and 16: Rep Rows 13 and 14.

Row 17: K1; *P1, (Dec 5, P3) twice, Dec 5, P1; rep from * to last st, K1.

Row18: Knit.

Repeat Rows 1 through 18 for pattern.

Dazzling Diamonds

Multiple: 6 + 7

STITCH GUIDE

M4: (K1, P1) twice in next st: 4 sts worked in one st.

K4 wrap: (K1, wrap yarn twice around needle) 3 times, K1.

INSTRUCTIONS

Note: *Slip all sl sts as if to purl.*

Row 1 (right side): K1; *P2, M4, P2, sl 1; rep from *, ending with P2, M4, P2, K1.

Row 2: K1; *K2, K4 wrap, K2, P1; rep from *, ending last rep with K2, K4 wrap, K3.

Row 3: K1; *P2, K4 dropping lps of each previously wrapped st, P2, sl 1; rep from *, ending with P2, K4 dropping lps of each previously wrapped st, P2, K1.

Row 4: K1; *K2, K4 wrap, K2, P1; rep from *, ending last rep with K2, K4 wrap, K3.

Row 5: K1; *P2, K4 dropping lps of each previously wrapped st, P2, sl 1; rep from *, ending with P2, K4 dropping lps of each previously wrapped st, P2, K1.

Row 6: K1; *K2, P4tog, K2, P1; rep from *, ending with K2, P4tog, K3.

Row 7: K1; *P2, sl 1, P2, M4; rep from *, ending with P2, sl 1, P2, K1.

Row 8: K1; *K2, P1, K2, K4 wrap; rep from *, ending with K2, P1, K3.

Row 9: K1; *P2, sl 1, P2, K4 dropping lps of each previously wrapped st; rep from *, ending with P2, sl 1, P2, K1.

Row 10: K1; *K2, P1, K2, K4 wrap; rep from *, ending with K2, P1, K3.

Row 11: K1; *P2, sl 1, P2, K4 dropping lps of each previously wrapped st; rep from *, ending with P2, sl 1, P2, K1.

Row 12: K1; *K2, P1, K2, P4tog; rep from *, ending with K2, P1, K3.

Repeat Rows 1 through 12 for pattern.

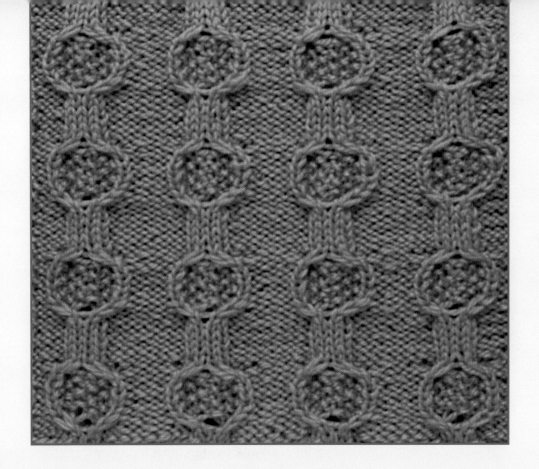

Dueling Banjoes

Multiple: 12 + 2

STITCH GUIDE

yfd (yarn forward): Bring yarn in front of needle: yfd made.

INSTRUCTIONS

Row 1: K1; *K4, P4, K4; rep from * to last st, K1.

Row 2 (right side): K1; *P4, K4, P4; rep from * to last st, K1.

Row 3: K1; *K4, P1, yfd, sl 2, P1, K4; rep from * to last st, K1.

Row 4: K1; *P2, sl next 3 sts to cn and hold at back, K1, then P1, K1, P1 from cable needle; sl next st to cn and hold at front, K1, P1, K1, then K1 from cn, P2; rep from * to last st, K1.

Row 5: K1; *K2, (P1, K1) 3 times, P2, K2; rep from * to last st, K1.

Row 6: K1; *P2, (K1, P1) 3 times, K2, P2; rep from * to last st, K1.

Rows 7 and 8: Rep Rows 5 and 6.

Rows 9 and 10: Rep Rows 5 and 6.

Row 11: K1; *K2, yfd, sl 1, (K1, P1) 3 times, yfd, sl 1, K2; rep from * to last st, K1.

Row 12: K1; *P2, sl next st to cn and hold at front, P2, K1, then K1 from cn; sl next 3 sts to cn and hold at back, K1, then K1, P2 from cn, P2; rep from * to last st, K1.

Rows 13 and 14: Rep Rows 1 and 2.

Rows 15 and 16: Rep Rows 13 and 14.

Repeat Rows 1 through 16 for pattern.

Hanging Bobbles

Multiple: 15 + 2

STITCH GUIDE

BB (Bobble): [(K1, P1) twice , K1] in next st, turn; P5, turn; K5, turn; P2tog, P1, P2tog, turn; sl 1, K2tog, PSSO: Bobble made.

FC (Front Cross): Sl one st to cn and hold in front, P1, then K1 from cn: FC made

BC (Back Cross): Sl one st to cn and hold at back, K1, then P1 from cn: BC made

M1P (Make 1 purl stitch): Pick up horizontal bar lying before next st and purl into back of this bar: increase made.

INSTRUCTIONS

Row 1 (right side): K1; *P15; rep from * to last st, K1.

Row 2: Knit.

Row 3: K1; *P7, BB, P7; rep from * to last st, K1.

Row 4: K1; *K7, P1, K7; rep from * to last st, K1.

Row 5: K1; *P4, BB, P2, K1 tbl, P2, BB, P4; rep from * to last st, K1.

Row 6: K1; *K4, P1, K2, P1, K2, P1, K4; rep from * to last st, K1.

Row 7: K1; *P2, BB, P1, FC, P1, K1 tbl, P1, BC, P1, BB, P2; rep from * to last st, K1.

Row 8: K1; *K2, P1, K2, (P1, K1) three times, K1, P1, K2; rep from * to last st, K1.

Row 9: K1; *P2, FC, P1, FC, K1 tbl, BC, P1, BC, P2; rep from * to last st, K1.

Row 10: K1; *K3, BC, K1, P3, K1, FC, K3; rep from * to last st, K1.

Row 11: K1; *P4, FC, M1P, sl 1, K2 tog, PSSO, M1P, BC, P4; rep from * to last st, K1.

Row 12: K1; *K5, BC, P1, FC, K5; rep from * to last st, K1.

Row 13: K1; *P5, purl into front and back of st, sl 1, K2tog, PSSO, purl into front and back of st, P5; rep from * to last st, K1.

Row 14: K1; K7, P1, K7; rep from * to last st, K1.

Repeat Rows 1 through 14 for pattern.

.

Tulips

Multiple: 21 + 2

STITCH GUIDE

SSK (slip, slip, knit): Slip next 2 sts as to knit, one at a time, to right needle; insert left needle into front of these 2 sts from right to left and then knit them tog: SSK made.

INSTRUCTIONS

Row 1 (right side): K1; *P10, K1, P10; rep from * to last st, K1.

Row 2: K1; *K10, P1, K10; rep from * to last st, K1.

Row 3: K1; *P9, K3, P9; rep from * to last st, K1.

Row 4: K1; *K9, P3, K9; rep from * to last st, K1.

Row 5: K1, *P8, K2, P1, K2, P8; rep from * to last st, K1.

Row 6: K1; *K8, P2, K1, P2, K8; rep from * to last st, K1.

Row 7: Rep Row 5.

Row 8: Rep Row 6.

Row 9: K1; *P7, K3, P1, K3, P7; rep from * to last st, K1.

Row 10: K1; * K7, P3, K1, P3, K7; rep from * to last st, K1.

Row 11: K1; *P7, (K3, P1, K3, sl these 7 sts to a dpn; wrap working yarn counter clockwise around sts twice; sl sts back to right hand needle), P7; rep from * to last st, K1.

Row 12: K1; *K7, P3, K1, P3, K7; rep from * to last st, K1.

Row 13: K1; *P6, K2tog, K2, YO, P1, YO, K2, SSK, P6; rep from * to last st, K1.

Row 14: K1; *K6, P4, K1, P4, K6; rep from * to last st, K1.

Row 15: K1; *P5, K2tog, K2, YO, K1, P1, K1, YO, K2, SSK, P5; rep from * to last st, K1.

Row 16: K1; *K5, P5, K1, P5, K5; rep from * to last st, K1.

Row 17: K1; P4, K2tog, K2, YO, K2, P1, K2, YO, K2, SSK, P4; rep from * to last st, K1.

Row 18: K1; *K4, P6, K1, P6, K4; rep from * to last st, K1.

Row 19: K1; *P3, K2tog, K2, YO, K2tog; K1, YO, P1, YO, K1, SSK, YO, K2, SSK, P3;rep from * to last st, K1.

Row 20: K1; *K3, P7, K1, P7, K3; rep from * to last st, K1.

Row 21: K1; *P2, K2tog, K2, YO, K2tog; K1, YO, P3, YO, K1, SSK, YO, K2, SSK, P2; rep from * to last st, K1.

Row 22: K1; *K2, P7, K3, P7, K2; rep from * to last st, K1.

Row 23: K1; *P2, YO, SSK, K1, K2tog, K1, YO, P5, YO, K1, SSK. K1, K2tog, YO, P2; rep from * to last st, K1.

Row 24: K1; *K2, P6, K5, P6, K2; rep from * to last st, K1.

Row 25: K1; *P4, K2tog, K1, YO, P7, YO, K1, SSK, P4; rep from * to last st, K1.

Row 26: K1; *K4, P3, K7, P3, K4; rep from * to last st, K1.

Repeat Rows 1 through 26 for pattern.

Climbing Leaves

Multiple: 25 +2

STITCH GUIDE

BC (Back Cross): Sl one st to cn and hold in back, K1 tbl, then P1 from cn: BC made.

FC (Front Cross): Sl 1 st to cn and hold in front, P1, then K1 tbl from cn: FC made

SKPO: Sl one st, K1 st, pass sl st over knit st: decrease made

M5 (Make 5 sts): [(K1, P1) twice, K1] into next st : 5 sts worked in one stitch.

INSTRUCTIONS

Row 1: K1; *K6, K2tog, YO, P3, K1 tbl, P1, K1 tbl, P3, YO, SKPO, K6; rep from * to last st, K1.

Row 2: K1; *P7, K4, P1, K1, P1, K4, P7; rep from * to last st, K1.

Row 3: K1; *YO, SKPO, K3, K2tog, YO, P2, K1 tbl, BC, P1, FC, K1 tbl, P2, YO, SKPO, K3, K2tog, YO; rep from * to last st, K1.

Row 4: K1; *K1, P5, K3, P2, K3, P2, K3, P5, K1; rep from * to last st, K1.

Row 5: K1; *P1, YO, SKPO, K1, K2tog, YO, P2, BC, K1 tbl, P1, M5, P1, K1 tbl, FC, P2, YO, SKPO, K1, K2tog, YO, P1; rep from * to last st, K1.

Row 6: K1; *K2, P3, K3, (P1, K1) twice, P5, (K1, P1) twice K3, P3, K2; rep from * to last st, K1.

Row 7: K1; *P2, YO, K3tog, YO, P2, BC, P1, K1 tbl, P1, K5, P1, K1 tbl, P1, FC, P2, YO, sl 1, K2tog, PSSO, YO, P2; rep from *to last st, K1.

Row 8: K1; *K3, P2, K2, P1, K2, P1, K1, P5, K1, P1, K2, P1, K2, P2, K3; rep from * to last st, K1.

Row 9: K1; *P4, K3tog, YO, K1, YO, P2, K1 tbl, P1, K5, P1, K1 tbl, P2, YO, K1, YO, sl 1, K2tog, PSSO, P4; rep from * to last st, K1.

Row 10: K1; *K4, P4, K2, P1, K1, P5, K1, P1, K2, P4, K4; rep from * to last st, K1.

Row 11: K1; *P2, K3tog, (K1, YO) twice, K1, P2, K1 tbl, P1, K2tog, K1, SKPO, P1, K1 tbl, P2, (K1, YO) twice, K1, sl 1, K2tog, PSSO, P2; rep from * to last st, K1.

Row 12: K1; *K2, P6, K2, P1, K1, P3tog, K1, P1, K2, P6, K2; rep from * to last st, K1.

Row 13: K1; *K3tog, K1, (K1, YO) twice, K2, P2, FC, P1, BC, P2, K1, (K1, YO) twice, K2, sl 1, K2tog, PSSO; rep from * to last st, K1.

Row 14: K1; *P8, K3, P3, K3, P8; rep from * to last st, K1.

Repeat Rows 1 through 14 for pattern.

Flowering Bush

Multiple: 11+ 7

STITCH GUIDE

C4F (Cable 4 Front): Sl 2 sts to cn and hold at front, K2, K2 from cn: C4F made.

C4B (Cable 4 Back): Sl 2 sts to cn and hold at back, K2, K2 from cn: C4B made.

BB (Bobble): [(K1, YO) twice, K1] into next st, turn; P5, turn; K5, pass 4th, 3rd, 2nd, and 1st sts separately over the last st knitted: BB made.

INSTRUCTIONS

Row 1 (right side): K1, purl to last st, K1.

Row 2: Knit.

Row 3: K1, P5; *C4B, P7; rep from * to last st, K1.

Row 4: K1; *K7, P4; rep from * to last 6 sts, K6.

Row 5: K1, P3; *C4B, C4F, P3; rep from * to last 3 sts, P2, K1.

Row 6: K6; *P8, K3; rep to last st, K1.

Row 7: K1, P3; *K8, P3; rep from * to last 3 sts, P2, K1.

Row 8: K6; *P8, K3; rep to last st, K1.

Row 9: K1, P3; *BB, K6, BB, P3; rep from * to last 3 sts, P2, K1.

Row 10: K6; *P8, K3; rep from * to last st, K1.

Row 11: K1, P5; *K4, P7; rep from * to last st, K1.

Row 12: K1; *K7, P4; rep from * to last 6 sts, K6.

Row 13: K1, P5; *BB, K2, BB, P7; rep from * to last st, K1.

Row 14: K1; *K7, P4, rep from * to last 6 sts, K6.

Repeat Rows 1 through 14 for pattern.

Puffs

Multiple: 10+ 4

INSTRUCTIONS

Row 1 (wrong side): K1; *purl to last st, K1.

Row 2: Knit.

Row 3: Rep Row 1.

Row 4: K2; *(K5, turn, P5, turn) 3 times; K10; rep from *, ending last rep with K2.

Row 5: Rep Row 1.

Row 6: Rep Row 2.

Row 7: Rep Row 1.

Row 8: K7; *(K5, turn, P5, turn) 3 times; K10; rep from * to last 7 sts; (K5, turn, P5) 3 times, K7.

Repeat Rows 1 through 8 for pattern.

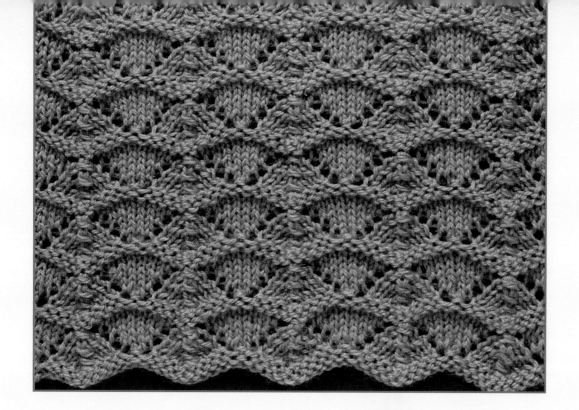

Rocky Road

Multiple: 10 + 2

INSTRUCTIONS

Note: *Sl st as if to knit.*

Row 1: K1, purl to last st, K1.

Row 2: Knit.

Row 3 (right side): K1; *YO, K3, sl 1, K2tog, PSSO, K3, YO, K1; rep from * to last st, K1.

Row 4 and all even rows: Rep Row 1.

Row 5: K1; *K1, YO, K2, sl 1, K2tog, PSSO, K2, YO, K2; rep from * to last st, K1.

Row 7: K1; *K2, YO, K1, sl 1, K2tog, PSSO, K1, YO, K3; rep from * to last st, K1.

Row 9: K1; *K3, YO, sl 1, K2tog, PSSO, YO, K4; rep from * to last st, K1.

Row 10: K1, purl to last st, K1.

Repeat Rows 1 through 10 for pattern, ending by working Row 2.

Cherry Tree

Multiple: 21+ 2

STITCH GUIDE

M1 (Make one stitch): Pick up horizontal bar lying before next st and knit into back of this bar: Increase made.

BB (Bobble): [(K1, YO) twice, K1] into next st; turn, P5; turn, K5; pass 4th, 3rd, 2nd, and 1st st separately over the last st knitted: BB made

INSTRUCTIONS

Row 1 (right side): Knit 1, purl to last st, K1.

Row 2: Knit.

Row 3: Rep Row 1.

Row 4: Rep Row 2.

Row 5: K1; *P4, K2tog, K3, M1, KI tbl, P1, KI tbl, MI, K3, sl 1, K1, PSSO, P4; rep from * to last st, K1.

Row 6: K1; *K4, P6, K1, P6, K4; rep from * to last st, K1.

Row 7: K1; *P3, K2tog, K3, M1, P1, K1 tbl, P1, K1 tbl, P1, M1, K3, sl 1, K1, PSSO, P3; rep from * to last st, K1.

Row 8: K1; *K3, P4, K2, P1, K1, P1, K2, P4, K3; rep from * to last st, K1.

Row 9: K1; *P2, K2tog, K3, M1, P2, KIB, P1, K1 tbl, P2, M1, K3, sl 1, K1, PSSO, P2; rep from * to last st, K1.

Row 10: K1; *K2, P4, K3, P1, K1, P1, K3, P4, K2; rep from * to last st, K1.

Row 11: K1; *P1, K2tog, K3, M1, P3, BB, P1, BB, P3, M1, K3, sl 1, K1, PSSO, P1; rep from * to last st, K1.

Row 12: K1; *K1, P5, K3, P1, K1, P1, K3, P5, K1; rep from * to last st, K1.

Row 13: K1; *K2tog, K3, M1, P3, (BB, P1) three times, P2, M1, K3, K2tog; rep from * to last st, K1.

Row 14: K1; *P4, K4, (P1, K1) 3 times, K3, P4; rep from * to last st, K1.

Row 15: K1; *K4, P3, (BB, P1) 4 times, P2, K4; rep from * to last st, K1.

Row 16: K1; *P4, K3, (P1, K1) 4 times, K2, P4; rep from * to last st, K1.

Row 17: K1; *K4, P4, (BB, P1) 3 times, P3, K4; rep from * to last st, K1.

Row 18: K1; *P4, K4, (P1, K1) 3 times, K3, P4; rep from * to last st, K1.

Row 19: K1; *K4, P5 (BB, P1) 2 times, P4, K4; rep from * to last st, K1.

Row 20: K1; *P4, K5, (P1, K1) 2 times, K4, P4; rep from * to last st, K1.

Row 21: K1, purl to last st, K1.

Row 22: Knit.

Repeat rows 3 through 22 for pattern.

Smocking

STITCH GUIDE

YB: yarn in back (on side of work away from you)

Multiple: 16 + 4

INSTRUCTIONS

Row 1 (wrong side): K3; *P2, K2; rep from * to last st, K1.

Row 2: K1, P2; *K2, P2; rep from * to last st, K1.

Row 3: K3; *P2, K2; rep from * to last st, K1.

Row 4: K1, P2; *YB, insert right needle from front between the next 6th and 7th sts on left needle and draw up a lp; sl lp onto left needle and knit it tog with first st on left needle; K1, P2, K2, P2; rep from * to last st, K1.

Row 5: Rep Row 1.

Row 6: Rep Row 2.

Row 7: Rep Row 1.

Row 8: K1, P2, K2; *P2, YB, insert right needle from front between the next 6th and 7th sts on left needle and draw up a lp; sl lp onto left needle and knit it tog with first st on left needle; K1, P2, K2; rep from * ending last rep with P2, K2, P2, K1.

Repeat Rows 1 through 8 for pattern.

40

Clusters

Multiple: 6 + 7

STITCH GUIDE

CLdec (Cluster Decrease): Sl 4 sts onto right needle, K1, pass each st separately over the knitted st: CLdec made.

M5 (Make 5): [(P1, K1) twice, P1] in same st: 5 sts worked in one st.

INSTRUCTIONS

Row 1: Knit.

Row 2: K1, purl to last st, K1.

Row 3: K4; *CLdec, K1; rep from *, ending with K3.

Row 4: K1, P3; *M5, P1; rep from *, ending with P2, K1.

Row 5: Knit.

Row 6: Rep Row 2.

Row 7: K1; *CLdec, *K1, CLdec; rep from * to last st, K1.

Row 8: K1, M5; *P1, M5; rep from * to last st, K1.

Repeat Rows 1 through 8 for pattern.

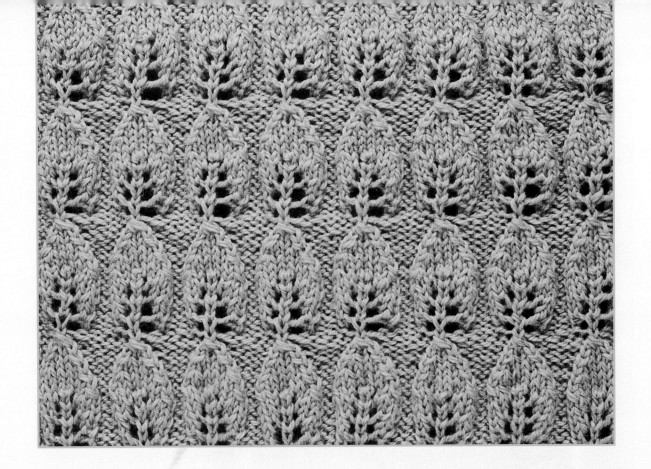

Leaves In A Row

Multiple: 5 + 2

INSTRUCTIONS

Row 1 (right side): K1; *P2, YO, K1, YO, P2; rep from * to last st, K1.

Row 2: K1; *K2, P3, K2; rep from * to last st, K1.

Row 3: K1; *P2, (K1, YO) twice, K1, P2; rep from * to last st, K1.

Row 4: K1; *K2, P5, K2; rep from * to last st, K1.

Row 5: K1; *P2, K2, (YO, K1) twice, K1, P2; rep from * to last st, K1.

Row 6: K1; *K2, P7, K2; rep from * to last st, K1.

Row 7: K1; *P2, K3, (YO, K1) twice, K2, P2; rep from * to last st, K1.

Row 8: K1; *K2, P9, K2; rep from * to last st, K1.

Row 9: K1; *P2, sl 1, K1, PSSO, K5, K2tog, P2; rep from * to last st, K1.

Row 10: K1; *K2, P7, K2; rep from * to last st, K1.

Row 11: K1; *P2, sl 1, K1, PSSO, K3, K2tog, P2; rep from * to last st, K1.

Row 12: K1; *K2, P5, K2; rep from * to last st, K1.

Row 13: K1; *P2, sl 1, K1, PSSO, K1, K2tog, P2; rep from * to last st, K1.

Row 14: K1; *K2, P3, K2; rep from * to last st, K1.

Row 15: K1; *P2, K3tog, P2; rep from * to last st, K1.

Row 16: K1; *K2, P1, K2; rep from * to last st, K1.

Repeat Rows 1 through 16 for pattern.

Birds in Flight

Multiple: 9 + 8

INSTRUCTIONS

Row 1 (wrong side): Knit.

Row 2: K4; *YO, K8, YO, K1; rep from * to last 4 sts, K4.

Row 3: K5; *P8, K3; rep from * to last 3 sts, K3.

Row 4: K5; *YO, K8, YO, K3; rep from * to last 3 sts, K3.

Row 5: K6; *P8, K5; rep from * to last 2 sts, K2.

Row 6: K6; *YO, K8, YO, K5; rep from * to last 2 sts, K2.

Row 7: K7; *P8, K7; rep from * to last st, K1.

Row 8: K7; *K4tog tbl, K4 tog, K7; rep from * to last st, K1.

Repeat Rows 1 through 8 for pattern, ending by working a Row 1.

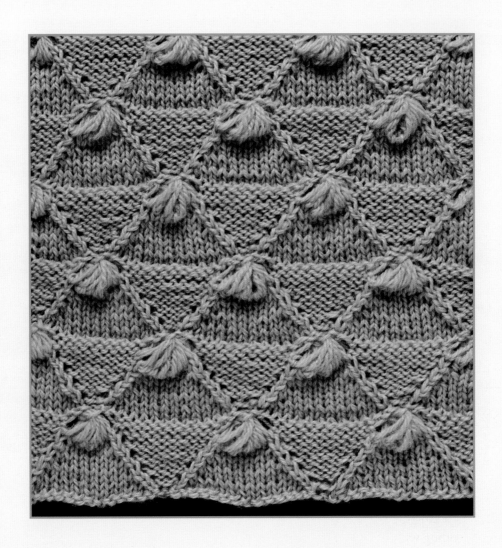

Diamond Puffs

Multiple: 16 + 3

STITCH GUIDE

M1 (Make one stitch): Pick up horizontal bar lying before next st and knit into back of this bar: Increase made.

YF: yarn in front (on side of work facing you)

INSTRUCTIONS

Row 1 (wrong side): K1, P1; *K15, P1; rep from * to last st, K1.

Row 2: K2; *M1, P2tog, P11, P2tog tbl, M1, K1; rep from * to last st, K1.

Row 3: K1, P2; *K13, P3; rep from *, ending last repeat with P2, K1.

Row 4: K3; *M1, P2tog, P9, P2tog tbl, M1, K3; rep from * across.

Row 5: K1, P3; *K11, P5; rep from *, ending with P3, K1.

Row 6: K4; *M1, P2tog, P7, P2tog tbl, M1, K5; rep from *, ending with K4.

Row 7: K1, P4: *K9, P7; rep from *, ending with P4, K1.

Row 8: K5; *M1, P2tog, P5, P2tog tbl, M1, K7; rep from *, ending with K5.

Row 9: K1, P5; *K7, P9; rep from *, ending with P5, K1.

Row 10: K6; *M1, P7 wrapping yarn 3 times after each st, M1, K9; rep from *, ending with K6.

Row 11: K1, P6; *YF, sl 7, dropping extra wraps, then insert left hand needle back into these 7 sts and P7tog, P11; rep from *, ending with P6, K1.

Row 12: K1, P6; *M1, K1, M1, P11; rep from *, ending with P6, K1.

Row 13: K8; *P1, K13; rep from *, ending with K8.

Row 14: K1, P7; *M1, K1, M1, P13; rep from *, ending with P7, K1.

Row 15: K8; *P3, K13; rep from *, ending with K8.

Row 16: K1, P5; *P2tog tbl, M1, K3, M1, P2tog, P9; rep from *, ending with P5, K1.

Row 17: K7; *P5, K11; rep from *, ending with K7.

Row 18: K1, P4; *P2tog tbl, M1, K5, M1, P2tog, P7; rep from *, ending with P4, K1.

Row 19: K6; *P7, K9; rep from *, ending with K6.

Row 20: K1, P3; *P2tog tbl, M1, K7, M1, P2tog, P5; rep from *, ending with P3, K1.

Row 21: K5; *P9, K7; rep from *, ending with K5.

Row 22: K1, P4 wrapping yarn 3 times after each st; *M1, K9, M1, P7 wrapping yarn 3 times for each st; rep from *, ending with P4 wrapping yarn three times for each st, K1.

Row 23: K1, YF, sl 4 dropping extra wraps, insert left-hand needle into these 4 sts and P4tog, *P11, YF, sl 7 dropping extra wraps, insert left-hand needle into these 7 sts and P7tog; rep from *, ending with YF, sl 4 dropping extra wraps, insert left-hand needle into these 4 sts and P4tog, K1.

Row 24: K1; *K1, M1, P11, M1; rep from *, ending with K2.

Row 25: K1, P1; *K13, P1; rep from *, ending with K1.

Row 26: K1; *K1, M1, P13, M1; rep from *, ending with K2.

Repeat Rows 3 through 26 for pattern.

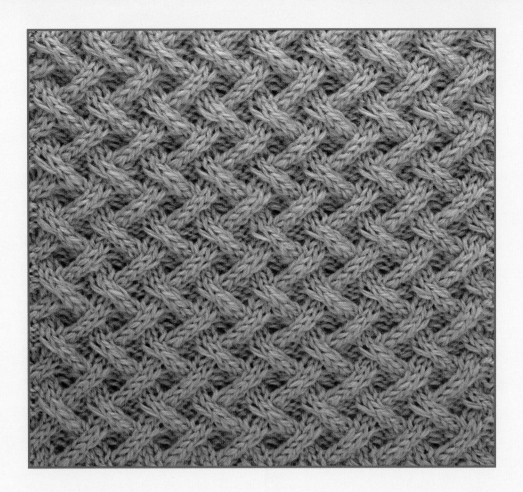

Lattice

Multiple: 6 + 10

STITCH GUIDE

C4F: Sl 2 sts to cn and hold at front, K2, K2 from cn: C4F made.

C4B: Sl 2 sts to cn and hold at back, K2, K2 from cn: C4B made.

TL (Twist Left): Sl 2 sts to cn and hold in front of work, P2, then K2 from cn: TL made.

TR (Twist Right): Sl 2 sts to cn and hold in back of work, K2, then P2 from cn: TR made.

INSTRUCTIONS

Row 1 (wrong side): K2; *K2, P4; rep from *, ending last rep with K2.

Row 2: K2; *C4F, P2; rep from *, ending last rep with K2.

Row 3: K2; *K2, P4; rep from *, ending last rep with K2.

Row 4: K2, P2; *K2, TR; rep from *, ending last rep with K6.

Row 5: K2; *P4, K2; rep from *, ending last rep with K2.

Row 6: K2; *P2, C4B; rep from *, ending last rep with K2.

Row 7: K2; *P4, K2; rep from *, ending last rep with K2.

Row 8: K6; *TL, K2; rep from * to last 4 sts, P2, K2.

Repeat Rows 1 through 8 for pattern.

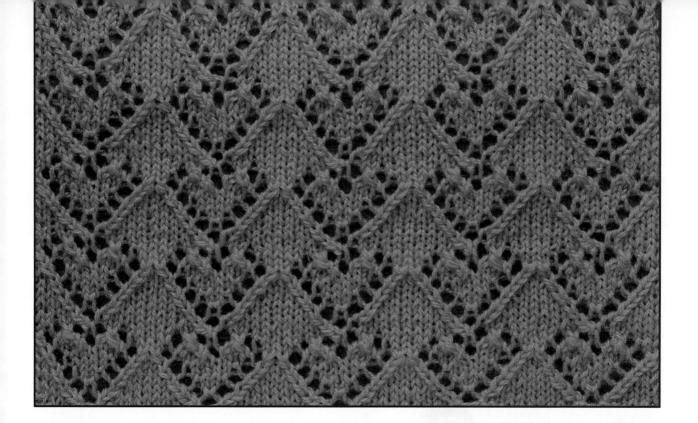

Hearts

Multiple: 11 + 2

STITCH GUIDE

SSK (slip, slip, knit): Slip next 2 sts as to knit one at a time to right needle; insert left needle into front of these 2 sts from right to left and then knit them tog: SSK made.

P2SSO (pass 2 sts over knit stitch): Slip 2 sts one at a time to right needle; then pass these 2 sl sts tog over knit stitch: P2SSO made.

INSTRUCTIONS

Row 1 (right side): K1; *K5, YO, SSK, K4; rep from * to last st, K1

Row 2 and all even rows: K1, purl to last st, K1.

Row 3: K1; * K3, K2tog, YO, K1, YO, SSK, K3; rep from * to last st, K1.

Row 5: K1; *K2, K2tog, YO, K3, YO, SSK, K2; rep from * to last st, K1.

Row 7: K1; *K1, K2tog, YO, K5, YO, SSK, K1; rep from * to last st, K1.

Row 9: K1; *K2tog, YO, K3, YO, K2tog, K2, YO, SSK; rep from * to last st, K1.

Row 11: K1; *K2, YO, sl 2, K1, P2SSO, YO, K1, YO, sl 2, K1, P2SSO, YO, K2; rep from * to last st, K1.

Row 12: Rep Row 2.

Repeat Rows 1 through 12 for pattern.

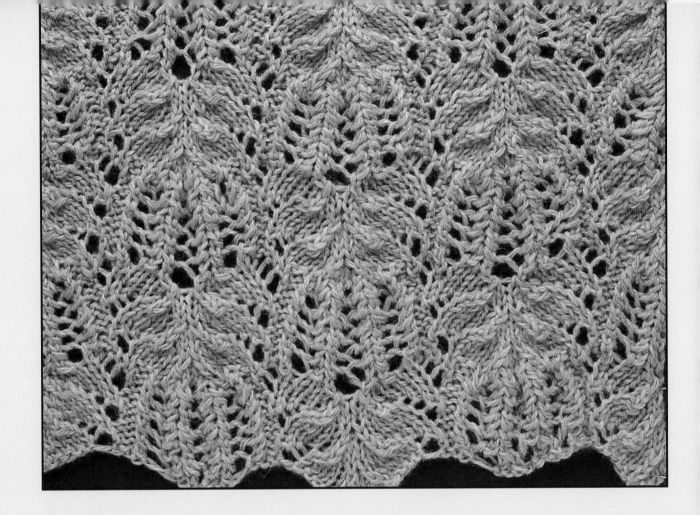

Spanish Lace

Multiple: 34 + 2

INSTRUCTIONS

Row 1 (right side): K1; *K3, K2tog, K4, YO, P2, (K2, YO, sl 1, K1, PSSO) 3 times, P2, YO, K4, sl 1, K1, PSSO, K3; rep from * to last st, K1.

Row 2: K1; *P2, P2tog tbl, P4, YO, P1, K2, (P2, YO, P2tog) 3 times, K2, P1, YO, P4, P2tog, P2; rep from * to last st, K1.

Row 3: K1; *K1, K2tog, K4, YO, K2, P2, (K2, YO, sl 1, K1, PSSO) 3 times, P2, K2, YO, K4, sl 1, K1, PSSO, K1; rep from * to last st, K1.

Row 4: K1; *P2tog tbl, P4, YO, P3, K2, (P2, YO, P2tog) 3 times, K2, P3, YO, P4, P2tog; rep from * to last st, K1.

Rows 5 through 8: Rep Rows 1 through 4.

Rows 9 through 12: Rep Rows 1 through 4.

Row 13: K1; *YO, sl 1, K1, PSSO, K2, YO, sl 1, K1, PSSO, P2, YO, K4, sl 1, K1, PSSO, K6, K2 tog, K4, YO, P2, K2, YO, sl 1, K1, PSSO, K2; rep from * to last st, K1.

Row 14: K1; *YO, P2tog, P2, YO, P2tog, K2, P1, YO, P4, P2tog, P4, P2tog tbl, P4, YO, P1, K2, P2, YO, P2tog, P2; rep from * to last st, K1.

Row 15: K1; *YO, sl 1, K1, PSSO, K2, YO, sl 1, K1, PSSO, P2, K2, YO, K4, sl 1, K1, PSSO, K2, K2tog, K4, YO, K2, P2, K2, YO, sl 1, K1, PSSO, K2; rep from * to last st, K1.

Row 16: K1; *YO, P2tog, P2, YO, P2tog, K2, P3, YO, P4, P2tog, P2tog tbl, P4, YO, P3, K2, P2, YO, P2tog, P2; rep from * to last st, K1.

Rows 17 through 20: Rep Rows 13 through 16.

Rows 21 through 24: Rep Rows 13 through 16.

Repeat Rows 1 through 24 for pattern.

Beehives

Multiple: 6 + 9

INSTRUCTIONS

Row 1 (right side): K1, purl to last st, K1.

Row 2: Knit.

Row 3 (and all odd rows): Rep Row 1.

Row 4: Knit.

Row 6: K1, P3tog, [(K1, P1) twice, K1] into next st; *P5tog, [(K1, p1)twice, K1] into next st; rep from * to last 4 sts, P3tog, K1.

Row 8: Knit.

Row 10: Knit.

Row 12: K1, (K1, P1, K1) into next st, P5tog; * [(K1, P1)twice, K1] into next st, P5tog; rep from * to last 2 sts, (K1, P1, K1) into next st, K1.

Row 14: Knit.

Repeat Rows 3 through 14 for pattern, ending by working Row 14.

Diamond Leaves

Multiple: 21 + 2

STITCH GUIDE

SKPO: Slip 1, knit 1, pass the slip stitch over the knit stitch: decrease made.

INSTRUCTIONS

Row 1 (wrong side): Knit.

Row 2 (right side): K1; *P10, K1, P10; rep from * to last st, K1.

Row 3: K1; *K9, P3, K9; rep from * to last st, K1.

Row 4: K1; *P8, K2tog, YO, K1, YO, SKPO, P8; rep from * to last st, K1.

Row 5: K1; *K8, P5, K8; rep from * to last st, K1.

Row 6: K1; P7, *K2tog, (K1, YO) twice, K1, SKPO, P7; rep from * to last st, K1.

Row 7: K1; *K7, P7, K7; rep from * to last st, K1.

Row 8: K1; *P6, K2tog, K2, (YO, K1) twice, K1, SKPO, P6; rep from * to last st, K1.

Row 9: K1; *K4, P13, K4; rep from * to last st, K1.

Row 10: K1; *P3, K2tog, YO, K1, YO, SKPO, K5, K2tog, YO, K1, YO, SKPO, P3; rep from * to last st, K1.

Row 11: K1; *K3, P15, K3; rep from * to last st, K1.

Row 12: K1; *P2, K2tog, (K1, YO) twice, K1, SKPO, K3, K2tog, (K1, YO) twice, K1, SKPO, P2; rep from * to last st, K1.

Row 13: K1; *K2, P17, K2; rep from * to last st, K1.

Row 14: K1; *P1, K2tog, K1, (K1, YO) twice, K2, K2tog, K1, SKPO, K1, (K1, YO) twice, K2, SKPO, P1; rep from * to last st, K1.

Row 15: K1; *K1, P19, K1; rep from * to last st, K1.

Row 16: K1; *P1, YO, SKPO, K5, K2tog, YO, K1, YO, SKPO, K5, K2tog, YO, P1; rep from * to last st, K1.

Row 17: K1; *K2, P17, K2; rep from * to last st, K1.

Row 18: K1; *P2, YO, SKPO, K3, K2tog, (K1, YO) twice, K1, SKPO, K3, K2tog, YO, P2; rep from * to last st, K1.

Row 19: K1; *K3, P15, K3; rep from * to last st, K1.

Row 20: K1; *P3, YO, SKPO, K1, K2tog, K2, (YO, K1) twice, K1, SKPO, K1, K2tog, YO, P3; rep from * to last st, K1.

Row 21: K1; *K4, P13, K4; rep from * to last st, K1.

Row 22: K1; *P4 (YO, SKPO) twice, K5, (K2tog, YO) twice, P4; rep from * to last st, K1.

Row 23: K1; *K7, P7, K7; rep from * to last st, K1.

Row24: K1; *P7, YO, SKPO, K3, K2tog, YO, P7; rep from * to last st, K1.

Row 25: K1; *K8, P5, K8; rep from * to last st, K1.

Row 26: K1: *P8, YO, SKPO, K1, K2tog, YO, P8; rep from * to last st, K1.

Row 27: K1; *K9, P3, K9; rep from * to last st, K1.

Row 28: K1; *P9, YO, K3tog, YO, P9; rep from * to last st, K1.

Repeat Rows 1 through 28 for pattern.

Chevron Bobbles

Multiple: 12 + 2

STITCH GUIDE

BB (Bobble): [(K1, P1) twice , K1 all into next st], turn: P5, turn; K5, pass 4th, 3rd, 2nd, and 1st st separately over the last st knitted: BB made.

INSTRUCTIONS

Row 1 (right side): K1; *K1 tbl, BB, (K1 tbl, P1) five times; rep from * to last st, K1.

Row 2 and all even rows: K1; *K1, P1; rep from * to last st, K1.

Row 3: K1; *K1 tbl, P1, K1 tbl, BB, (K1 tbl, P1) three times, K1 tbl, BB; rep from * to last st, K1.

Row 5: K1; *(K1 tbl, P1) twice, K1 tbl, BB, K1 tbl, P1, K1 bl, BB, K1 tbl, P1; rep from * to last st, K1.

Row 7: K1; *(K1 tbl, P1) three times, K1 tbl, BB, (K1 tbl, P1) twice; rep from * to last st, K1.

Row 8: Rep Row 2.

Repeat Rows 1 through 8 for pattern.

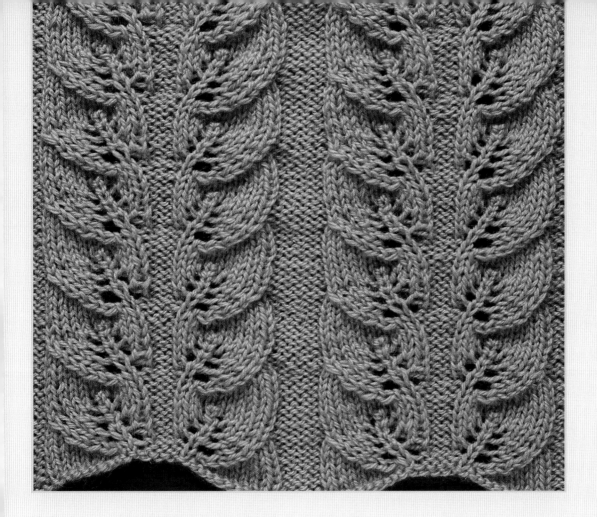

Leafy Columns

Multiple: 30+2

INSTRUCTIONS

Row 1 (right side): K1; *P3, K10, P4, K10, P3; rep from * to last st, K1.

Row 2 and all even rows: K1;*K3, P10, K4, P10, K3; rep from * to last st, K1.

Row 3: K1; *P3, K6, K3tog, YO, K1, YO, P4, YO, K1, YO, sl 1, K2tog, PSSO, K6, P3; rep from * to last st, K1.

Row 5: K1; *P3, K4, K3tog, K1, YO, K1, YO, K1, P4, K1, YO, K1, YO, K1, sl 1, K2tog, PSSO, K4, P3; rep from * to last st, K1.

Row 7: K1; *P3, K2, K3tog, K2, YO, K1, YO, K2, P4, K2, YO, K1, YO, K2, sl 1, K2tog, PSSO, K2, P3; rep from * to last st, K1.

Row 9: K1; *P3, K3tog, K3, YO, K1, YO, K3, P4, K3, YO, K1, YO, K3, sl 1, K2tog, PSSO, P3; rep from * to last st, K1.

Row 10: Rep Row 2.

Repeat Rows 1 through 10 for pattern.

Petticoats

Multiple: 21+ 2

STITCH GUIDE

FC (Front Cross): Sl one st to cn and hold in front; P1, K1 from cn: FC made.

BC (Back Cross): Sl one st to cn and hold in back; K1, P1 from cn: BC made.

BB (Bobble): (K1, P1) twice into next st, turn; P4, turn; K4, pass 3rd, 2nd, and 1st stitch separately over the last st knitted: BB made.

INSTRUCTIONS

Row 1 (right side): K1; *P2, (BB, P3) 4 times, BB, P2; rep from * to last st, K1.

Row 2: K1; *K2, P1, (K3, P1) 4 times, K2; rep from * to last st, K1.

Row 3: K1; *P2, (K1, P3) 4 times, K1, P2; rep from * to last st, K1.

Row 4: K1; *K2, P1, (K3, P1) 4 times, K2; rep from * to last st, K1.

Row 5: K1; *P2, FC, P2, (K1, P3) twice, K1, P2, BC, P2; rep from * to last st, K1.

Row 6: K1; *K3, P1, K2, (P1, K3) twice, P1, K2, P1, K3; rep from * to last st, K1.

Row 7: K1; *P3, K1, P2, (K1, P3) twice, K1, P2, K1, P3; rep from * to last st, K1.

Row 8: K1; *K3, P1, K2, (P1, K3) twice, P1, K2, P1, K3; rep from * to last st, K1.

Row 9: K1; *P3, FC, P1, FC, P2, K1, P2, BC, P1, BC, P3; rep from * to last st, K1.

Row 10: K1; *K4, P1 (K2, P1) four times, K4; rep from * to last st, K1.

Row 11: K1; *P4, (K1, P2) five times, P2; rep from * to last st, K1.

Row 12: K1; *K4, (P1, K2) four times, P1, K4; rep from * to last st, K1.

Row 13: K1; *P4, FC, P1, (K1, P2) twice, K1, P1, BC, P4; rep from * to last st, K1.

Row 14: K1; *K5, P1, K1 (P1, K2) twice, P1, K1, P1, K5; rep from * to last st, K1.

Row 15: K1; *P5, K1, P1, (K1, P2) twice, K1, P1, K1, P5; rep from * to last st, K1.

Row 16: K1; *K5, P1, K1, P1 (K2, P1) twice, K1, P1, K5; rep from * to last st, K1.

Row 17: K1; *P5, (FC) twice, P1, K1, P1, (BC) twice, P5; rep from * to last st, K1.

Row 18: K1; *K6, (P1, K1) four times, P1, K6; rep from * to last st, K1.

Row 19: K1; *P6, (K1, P1) four times, K1, P6; rep from * to last st, K1.

Row 20: K1; *K6, (P1, K1) four times, P1, K6; rep from * to last st, K1.

Row 21: K1; *P6, insert right needle from front between 15th and 16th sts on left needle and draw through a lp; sl this lp onto left needle and knit it tog with first st on left needle; (P1, K1) four times, P6; rep from * to last st, K1.

Row 22: K1; *K6, (P1, K1) four times, P1, K6; rep from * to last st, K1.

Repeat Rows 1 through 22 for pattern.

Arrowheads

Multiple: 13 + 2

STITCH GUIDE

BB (Bobble): (K1, P1, K1) into next st, turn; P3, turn; K3, turn; P3, turn; sl 1, K2tog, PSSO: BB made.

INSTRUCTIONS

Row 1 (right side): K1; *P4, K5, P4; rep from * to last st, K1.

Row 2: K1; *K4, P5, K4; rep from * to last st, K1.

Row 3: K1; *P3, K2tog, K1, (YO, K1) twice, K2tog tbl, P3; rep from * to last st, K1.

Row 4: K1; *K3, P7, K3; rep from * to last st, K1.

Row 5: K1; *P2, K2tog, K1, YO, K3, YO, K1, K2tog tbl, P2; rep from * to last st, K1.

Row 6: K1; *K2, P9, K2; rep from * to last st, K1.

Row 7: K1; *P1, K2tog, K1, YO, K5, YO, K1, K2tog tbl, P1; rep from * to last st, K1.

Row 8: K1; *K1, P11, K1; rep from * to last st, K1.

Row 9: K1; *K2tog, K1, YO, K3, BB, K3, YO, K1, K2tog tbl; rep from * to last st, K1.

Row 10: K1, purl to last st, K1.

Repeat Rows 1 through 10 for pattern, ending wth Row 10.

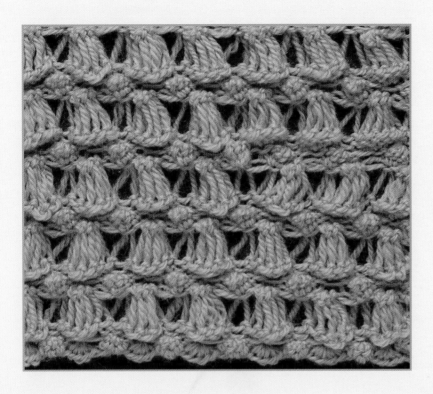

Little Bells

Multiple 6 + 2

STITCH GUIDE

M5 (Make 5): (K1, YO, K1, YO, K1) in same st: 5 sts in one made.

INSTRUCTIONS

Row 1: K1; *P5tog, M5 in next st; rep from * to last st, K1.

Row 2 (right side): K1; Purl to last st, K1.

Row 3: K1; *M5 in next st, P5 tog; rep from * to last st, K1.

Row 4: Rep Row 2.

Row 5: K1; *K1, wrapping thread 3 times around needle for each stitch; rep from * to last st, K1.

Row 6: K1; *P1, letting extra lps drop off needle; rep from * to last st, K1.

Repeat Rows 1 through 6, ending by working Row 2.

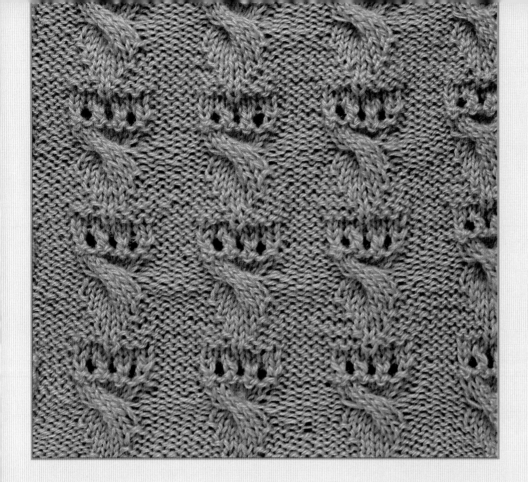

Tassels

Multiple: 12 + 2

INSTRUCTIONS

Row 1 (right side): K1; *P3, K1, P8; rep from * to last st, K1.

Row 2: K1; *K8, P1, K3; rep from * to last st, K1.

Row 3: K1; *P2, K3, P7; rep from * to last st, K1.

Row 4: K1; *K7, P3, K2; rep from * to last st, K1.

Row 5: K1; *P1, K5, P6; rep from * to last st, K1.

Row 6: K1; *K6, P5, K1; rep from * to last st, K1.

Row 7: K1; *K7, P5; rep from * to last st, K1.

Row 8: K1 *K5, P7; rep from * to last st, K1.

Rows 9 through 12: Rep Rows 7 and 8.

Row 13: K1; *Sl next 3 sts onto a cn and hold at front, K4, K3 from cn, P5; rep from * to last st, K1.

Row 14: K1; *K5, P7; rep from * to last st, K1.

Row 15: K1; *K7, P5; rep from * to last st, K1.

Row 16: Knit.

Row 17: K1; *K1, (YO, K2tog) 3 times, P5; rep from * to last st, K1.

Row 18: K1; * K5, P7; rep from * to last st, K1.

Row 19: K1; *K7, P5; rep from * to last st, K1.

Row 20: K1; *K5, P7; rep from * to last st, K1.

Repeat Rows 1 through 20 for pattern.

Flowering Vine

Multiple: 21 + 2

STITCH GUIDE

Cross 5 left (Cr5L): Sl 3 sts to cn and hold in front, P2, K3 from cn: Cr5L made.

Cross 4 left (Cr4L): Sl 3 sts to cn and hold in front, P1, K3 from cn: Cr4L made.

Cross 4 right (Cr4R): Sl one st to cn and hold in back, K3, P1 from cn: Cr4R made.

Cross 3 left (Cr3L): Sl 2 sts to cn and hold in front, P1, then K2 from cn: Cr3L made.

Back Cross (BC): Sl one st to cn and hold at back, K1, P1 from cn: BC made.

Front Cross (FC): Sl one st to cn and hold in front, P1, then K1 from cn: FC made.

Make 1 (M1): Pick up horizontal bar between next 2 sts with left needle and knit into back of st: inc made.

SKPO: Sl 1, K1, pass sl st over knit st: decrease made.

Bobble (BB): [(K1, YO) twice, K1] into next st; turn, P5; turn, K5; pass 4th, 3rd, 2nd, and 1st st separately over the last st knitted: BB made.

INSTRUCTIONS

Row 1 (right side): K1; *P9, K3, P9; rep from * to last st, K1.

Row 2: K1; *K9, P3, K9; rep from * to last st, K1.

Row 3: K1; *P9, Cr5L, P7; rep from * to last st, K1.

Row 4: K1; *K7, P3, K11; rep from * to last st, K1.

Row 5: K1; *P3, BB, P7, Cr5L, P5; rep from * to last st, K1.

Row 6: K1; *K5, P3, K13; rep from * to last st, K1.

Row 7: K1; *P2, BB, K1, BB, P4, BB, P3, Cr5L, P3; rep from * to last st, K1.

Row 8: K1; *K3, P4, K9, P1, K4; rep from * to last st, K1.

Row 9: K1; *P4, FC, P2, BB, K1, BB, P3, K1, Cr5L, P1; rep from * to last st, K1.

Row 10: K1; *K1, P3, K2, P1, K4, P1, K3, P1, K5; rep from * to last st, K1.

Row 11: K1; *P5, (FC, P2) twice, BC, P2, K3, P1; rep from * to last st, K1.

Row 12: K1; *K1, P3, K3, P1, K2, P1, K3, P1, K6; rep from * to last st, K1.

Row 13: K1; *P5, BC, P2, BC, P1, (K1, YO) twice, K1, P2, Cr4L; rep from * to last st, K1.

Row 14: K1; *P3, K5, P1, K4, P1, K3, P1, K5; rep from * to last st, K1.

Row 15: K1; *P5, FC, P1, BC, P2, K2, YO, K1, YO, K2, P3, K3; rep from * to last st, K1.

Row 16: K1; *P3, K3, P7, K3, P1, K1, P1, K6; rep from * to last K1.

Row 17: K1; *P6, FC, K1, P3, SKPO, K3, K2tog, P3, K3; rep from * to last st, K1.

Row 18: K1; *P3, K3, P5, K3, P2, K7; rep from * to last st, K1.

Row 19: K1; *P6, K3, P3, SKPO, K1, K2tog, P2, Cr4R; rep from * to last st, K1.

Row 20: K1; *K1, P3, K2, P3, K3, P3, K6; rep from * to last st, K1.

Row 21: K1; *P5, BC, K2, P3, M1, K3tog, M1, P1, Cr4R, P1; rep from * to last st, K1.

Row 22: K1; *K2, P3, K7, P2, K1, P1, K5; rep from * to last st, K1.

Row 23: K1; *P4, K1, (YO, K1) twice, Cr3L, P5, Cr4R, P2; rep from * to last st, K1.

Row 24: K1; *K3, P3, K5, P2, K1, P5, K4; rep from * to last st, K1.

Row 25: K1; *P4, K2, YO, K1, YO, K2, P1, Cr3L, P3, Cr4R, P3; rep from * to last st, K1.

Row 26: K1; *K4, P3, K3, P2, K2, P7, K4; rep from * to last st, K1.

Row 27: K1; *P4, K7, P2, Cr3L, P1, Cr4R, P4; rep from * to last st, K1.

Row 28: K1; *K5, P3, K1, P2, K3, P7, K4; rep from * to last st, K1.

Row 29: K1; *P4, SKPO, K3, K2tog, P3, Cr3L, K3, P5; rep from * to last st, K1.

Row 30: K1; *K5, P5, K4, P5, K4; rep from * to last st, K1.

Row 31: K1; *P4, SKPO, K1, K2tog, P5, K3, P6; rep from * to last st, K1.

Row 32: K1; *K6, P3, K5, P3, K4; rep from * to last st, K1.

Row 33: K1; *P4, M1, K3tog, M1, P4, Cr4R, P6; rep from * to last st, K1.

Row 34: K1; *K7, P3, K11; rep from * to last st, K1.

Row 35: K1; *P10, Cr4R, P7; rep from * to last st, K1.

Row 36: K1; *K8, P3, K10; rep from * to last st, K1.

Row 37: K1; *P9, Cr4R, P8; rep from * to last st, K1.

Row 38: K1; *K9, P3, K9; rep from * to last st, K1.

Repeat Rows 1 through 38 for pattern.

Hugs and Kisses

Multiple: 16 + 2

STITCH GUIDE

C4F (Cable 4 Front): Sl 2 sts to cn and hold at front, K2, K2 from cn: C4F made.

C4B (Cable 4 Back): Sl 2 sts to cn and hold at back, K2, K2 from cn: C4B made.

INSTRUCTIONS

Row 1 (right side): Knit.

Row 2 and all even rows: K1, purl to last st, K1.

Row 3: K1; *C4B, (C4F) twice, C4B; rep from * to last st, K1.

Row 5: Rep Row 1.

Row 7: K1; *C4B, (C4F) twice; C4B; rep from * to last st, K1.

Row 9: Rep Row 1,

Row 11: K1; *C4F, (C4B) twice, C4F; rep from * to last st, K1.

Row 13: Rep Row 1.

Row 15: K1; *C4F, (C4B) twice, C4F; rep from * to last st, K1.

Row 16: Rep Row 2.

Repeat Rows 1 through 16 for pattern.

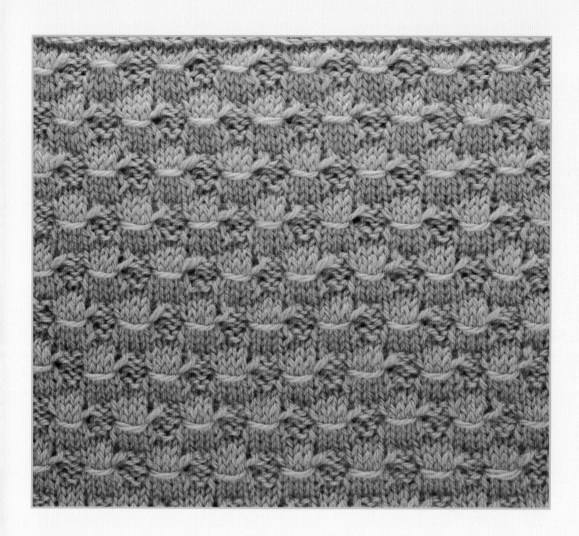

Sheaves of Wheat

Multiple: 6+3

STITCH GUIDE

Wrap: With yarn in back, insert right needle between next 4th and 5th sts on left needle; K1, drawing up longer lp than usual, K4; sl one strand of long st over 4 sts to wrap them: wrap made.

INSTRUCTIONS

Row 1 (right side): K1; *K4, P2; rep from *, ending with K2.

Row 2: P2; *K2, P4; rep from * to last st, K1.

Row 3: K1; *Wrap, P2; rep from *, ending last rep with K2.

Row 4: K1, P1; *K2, P4; rep from * to last st, K1.

Row 5: Knit.

Row 6: K1, purl to last st, K1.

Row 7: K2; *P2, K4; rep from * to last st, K1.

Row 8: K1; *P4, K2; rep from *, ending last rep with P1, K1.

Row 9: K2; *P2, Wrap; rep from * to last st, K1.

Row 10: K1; *P4, K2; rep from *, ending last rep wth P1, K1.

Row 11: Knit.

Row 12: Rep Row 6.

Repeat Rows 1 through 12 for pattern.

Scallops

Multiple: 21 + 3.

INSTRUCTIONS

Row 1: Knit.

Row 2 (right side): K1, purl to last st, K1.

Row 3: Knit.

Row4: K1; *YO, K21; rep from * to last 2 sts; K2.

Row 5: K1, P1; *(P1, K3) 5 times, P2; rep from * to last st; K1.

Row 6: K1 *K1, YO, K1, (P3, K1) 5 times; YO; rep from *to last 2 sts; K2.

Row 7: K1, P1; *P2, (K3, P1) 5 times, P2; rep from * to last st; K1.

Row 8: K1; *(K1, YO) twice; (sl 1 as to knit, K1, PSSO, P2) 5 times; (K1, YO) twice; rep from * to last 2 sts, K2.

Row 9: K1, P1; *P4, (K2, P1) 5 times; P4; rep from * to last st; K1.

Row 10: K1; *(K1, YO) 4 times; (sl 1 as to knit, K1, PSSO, P1) 5 times; (K1, YO) 4 times; rep from * to last 2 sts; K2.

Row 11: K1, P1; *P8, (Kl, P1) 5 times; P8; rep from * to last st; K1.

Row 12: K1; *K8, (sl 1 as to knit, K1, PSSO) 5 times; K8; rep from * to last 2 sts; K2.

Row 13: K1, P1; *P8, P4, slip the 4 sts just made from right-hand needle to cn, wrap yarn around all 4 sts clockwise 3 times; slip same 4 sts back to right hand needle, P9; rep from * to last st; K1.

Row 14: Knit.

Repeat Rows 1 through 14, ending by working a Row 2.

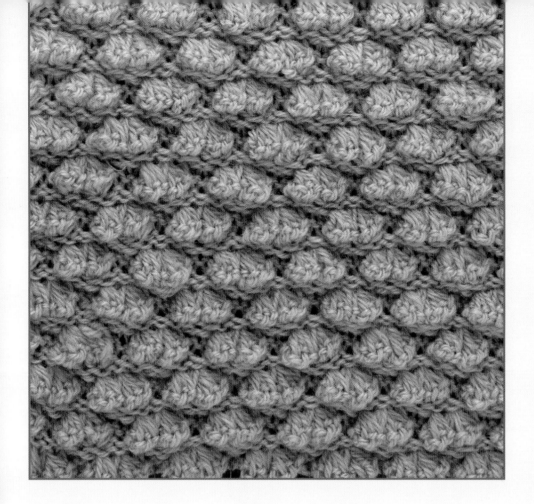

Puffys

Multiple: 4 + 4

STITCH GUIDE

M5: (P1, K1) twice, P1 in same stitch: 5 stitches made in one stitch.

LS (Long Stitch): K1, wrapping yarn twice around needle.

INSTRUCTIONS

Row 1 (right side): K1, P2; *(M5) twice; P2; rep from * to last st, K1.

Row 2: K3; *(LS)10 times; K2; rep from * to last st, K1.

Row 3: K1, P2; *(sl 5 LS to right needle, allowing extra lps to drop; return sts to left needle and K5 tog through back lp) twice; P2; rep from * to last st, K1.

Row 4: Knit.

Row 5: K1, P1; *M5, P2, M5; rep from * to last 2 sts, P1, K1.

Row 6: K2, *(LS) 5 times, K2, (LS) 5 times; rep from * to last 2 sts, K2.

Row 7: K1, P1, *sl 5 LS to right needle, allowing extra lps to drop; return sts to left needle and K5tog through back lp; P2; sl 5 LS to right needle, allowing extra lps to drop; return sts to left needle and K5 through back lp; rep from * to last 2 sts, P1, K1.

Row 8: Knit.

Repeat Rows 1 through 8 for pattern.

General Directions

ABBREVIATIONS AND SYMBOLS

Knit patterns are written in a special shorthand, which is used so that instructions don't take up too much space. They sometimes seem confusing, but once you learn them, you'll have no trouble following them.

These are Standard Abbreviations

BB	bobble
Beg	beginning
Cn	cable needle
Cont	continue
Dec	decrease
Dpn	double point needle
Inc	increase(ing)
K	knit
K2tog	knit two stitches together
K4tog	knit four stitches together
Lp(s)	loop(s)
LS	long stitch
M1	Increase one stitch
M5	Increase five stitches
P	purl
P2tog	purl two stitches together
P3tog	purl three stitches together
P4tog	purl four stitches together
P5tog	purl five stitches together
Patt	pattern
Prev	previous
PSSO	pass the slipped stitch over
P2SSO	pass 2 sts over knit st
Rem	remain(ing)
Rep	repeat(ing)
Sk	skip
SKPO	slip 1, knit 1, pass slip stitch over knit st
Sl	slip
SPPO	sl 1, purl 1, pass slip stitch over purl st
SSK	slip, slip, knit
St(s)	stitch(es)
Tbl	through back loop
Tog	together
YB	yarn in back of needle
YF	yarn in front of needle
YO	Yarn over the needle
YRN	Yarn around needle

These are Standard Symbols

* An asterisk (or double asterisks**) in a pattern row, indicates a portion of instructions to be used more than once. For instance, "rep from * three times" means that after working the instructions once, you must work them again three times for a total of 4 times in all.

( ) Parentheses enclose instructions which are to be worked the number of times following the parentheses. For instance, "(K1, P2) 3 times" means that you knit one stitch and then purl two stitches, three times.

[ ] Brackets are used in the same way as parentheses especially when there is more than one set of repeats such as [(K1, P1)twice, K5] 3 times.